The Hidden Treasue of the Holy Mass

by St. Leonard of Port Maurice

IN THE WORLD YOU WILL HAVE AFFLICTION.
BUT TAKE COURAGE,

I HAVE OVERCOME THE WORLD.

– JOHN 16:33

Contents

Allegory of the Holy Sacrament by Juan Correa, 1690

Introduction

Some time ago, a religious superior, whose works have been specially blessed by our dear Lord, asked for a translation of the following book. The version now presented to the public was undertaken at my request by a Catholic layman; and as the coadjutor Bishop of the Western District of Scotland has kindly revised it, I am glad to be allowed to cooperate with this venerable Prelate in recommending it to the perusal of Catholics.

If St. Philip Neri was satisfied with a book when the name of its author began with S, it will be surely unnecessary to recommend this treatise, which bears the name of the heroic missionary, Saint Leonard of Port Maurice. To those who have read his *Life* it must appear strange how he found time, in the course of his apostolic wanderings, to compose his various works. Reviewing his efforts to gain souls, his retreats, his sermons, his journeys, they will conclude that his support under such labors must have been in the Holy Sacrifice of the Mass; and they will not wonder that he has spoken with so much unction of its efficacy and graces. Where could he, after hours spent in the confessional, hours short for his zeal, but long for his bodily strength, find vigor, save in the refreshing waters for which, as he said in his daily preparation, he thirsted as the stag thirsts after the fountains of water? To him Our Lord was truly the strong and the living God, and from Him he received each day power to begin anew the fight which ended only when he went to receive his crown. While the holy missionary was collecting the faithful to the Stations of the Cross in the Coliseum, he may, perhaps, have looked to the building on the neighboring hill where his earthly remains were to await the resurrection, and felt in ardent faith that the Sacrifice which those Stations commemorated was really and truly offered on the altars of that humble church. And then his heart would bum with the desire to make all Christians love the Lamb Whom his faith beheld „standing as if slain," *stantem tanquam occisum* (Apoc. v. 6), and he would wish to make men understand how certainly this blessed Victim offers for our sake, day after day, the

Sacrifice of Mount Calvary.

We think that if we had lived with Mary and the Apostles, we should have loved Him really. If so, when the Fathers tell us that in the Blessed Sacrament He perpetuates and continues the Incarnation for us, we ought to show this love; and where is it? When we have to bear the reproach of our many sins, we persuade ourselves that we should not have committed them if we had knelt with John under the Cross; and yet in the Mass the very same Sacrifice is before our eyes, while we too often remain as hardened as ever. But Saint Leonard saw that it would be at least difficult for men to remain in their sins if they were drawn often to this Sacrifice, by the offering whereof, as the Council of Trent teaches, „the Lord being appeased, sends grace and the gift of repentance, and forgives crimes and even grievous sins." Therefore, he sought to draw them to the altar, and bade them pray for the grace that cannot fail. More than once it has happened that those who were not Catholics have been converted by being present during Mass: and can we wonder at it when He, Whose look converted Peter, looks upon them from the altar? Some there are, favored souls and fervent in prayer, who cannot hear Mass without tears. No one ever saw the holy Pontiff Gregory XVI in the presence of the Blessed Sacrament without witnessing the tenderness to which he was moved.

If we had but faith, we should see the heavenly host gathered around the altar during Mass, „since," as the Council of Oxford says, „it is undoubted that the whole heavenly court is then present." (*Anno* 1222.) When the prophet prayed, the eyes of his servant were opened, and he saw the hill covered with fiery chariots (4 Kings vi. 17); and if the holy author of this book would pray that we might see the altar as he saw it, our eyes, opened to the light which is there shining (*in lumine tuo videbimus lumen*), would behold the chariots of fire on which the heavenly host are borne when their King comes from His throne to earth. If some pious person possessing worldly means were to see the picture designed in explanation of Mass by M. Olier, the devout leader of the Sulpicians, we think he would be disposed to fulfill the intention which death prevented that holy man from carrying out, by having the picture engraved, and scattered among the faithful. The picture is in itself a meditation, and a sermon upon the mysterious presence of the

9

Saints and Angels with their glorious Queen during the Holy Sacrifice, upon the graces which flow from the altar over the whole Church, and upon its ineffable comfort to our suffering brethren in Purgatory. We venture to extract from the Life of M. Olier a description of this picture; and while we are reading it, let us remember that such is the Mass every time it is offered, rendering glory to Heaven, pouring grace upon the earth, and shedding consolation over Purgatory.

„When the priest celebrates," says the author of the *Imitation*, „he honors God, he rejoices the Angels, he edifies the Church, he helps the living, he obtains repose for the dead." (iv, v., 3.) This is the subject which M. Olier wished to represent in this picture. At the moment of the Elevation, the Church Triumphant, borne on the clouds, descends, and unites herself to the Church on earth, to be an offering to God, as one sole victim with Jesus Christ.

„In the upper part we see God the Father, to Whom the Sacrifice is offered. He contemplates the holy Victim Who immolates Himself to His glory, and He seems to accept the oblation with infinite complacency and satisfaction. The most holy Virgin is placed a little lower; she kneels, as do all the Saints and Angels, to show their dependence in respect of the Creator; nevertheless, she addresses God with the confidence of a Spouse, and seems to exercise that suppliant almightiness which the holy doctors recognize in the august Queen of Heaven.

„The celestial spirits, ranged around the God Whom they adore by Jesus Christ, are divided into three hierarchies, of which each is made to contain three orders, forming altogether the nine choirs of Angels; at their head we see St. Michael, then the angel Gabriel, who bends toward Mary. The holy Precursor is alone, on account of his greatness, among the children of men. „Next we see, on one side, Adam and Eve, and the just of the law of nature; and, on the other, Moses with the Saints of the Mosaic Law, who, in transports of gratitude, confess that they have obtained salvation through the blood of Jesus Christ alone, the sole virtue of all the ancient sacrifices. These are headed by the prophet David, placed thus near to Mary and St. Joseph, as being their ancestor. „The next portion of the picture is the Christian Church, in three orders, or circles. The holy Apostles appear in the first ----- they who, triumphing over idolatry, shed over the world the knowledge of God. St. Peter, their chief, returns thanks to the Eternal Father for having inspired him to make the immortal confession which was the origin of his prerogatives; St. Paul blesses Him for having called him to the apostolate (Gal. i. 1); and St. James the Great, for having given him a place in His kingdom (St. Matt. xx. 23). Close to St. Peter we get a glimpse of St. John, placed nearer to God, Whose highest mysteries he seemed to penetrate, and next to the most holy Virgin, to whom he was given as a son and a guardian. St. Andrew, St. Thomas, and St. Bartholomew come next, each designated by the instruments of his Martyrdom; and then the other Apostles, the disciples, and the preachers of the Faith. Opposite are the holy Martyrs, triumphant over their persecutors: they return thanks to God by Jesus Christ, their invisible strength, and renew their offering in union with His. Their leader, St. Stephen, seems still continuing his sacrifice: we recognize several of the most illustrious Martyrs following him ----- St. Domitella, St. Laurence, St. Cecilia, St. Vincent, St. Barbara, St. Agnes. „In the second rank we see, on one side, the holy doctors; at their head, St. Leo, St. Gregory the Great, St. Ambrose, and St. Augustine; they all give thanks to God for the victories they have gained over heresies, through Jesus Christ, the sole source of their enlightenment. On the other side are all the holy monks and nuns, represented by their founders, each in the habit of his order; they glorify God for having enabled them to overcome the love of the goods of this world, by true poverty, and for having chosen them to represent to the Church, according to their respective institutes, some virtue, or some hidden perfection, of Jesus Christ. They are placed in the following order: St. Benedict, considered as patriarch of the Western Monks; an old religious of the Carmelite Order; next, St. Teresa, in the habit of her reform; St. Scholastica, as mother of the Benedictines; St. Bernard, restorer of the Cistercian Order; a Cistercian nun; a monk of Cluny, arrayed in black; St. Francis of Assisi, founder of the Friars Minor; St. Claire, foundress of the Poor Clares; then St. Bruno, patriarch of the Carthusians; St. Dominic, founder of the Friars Preachers; St. Francis of Paula, founder of the Minorities; St. Ignatius Loyola; and various societies of regular clerks.

„Finally, the laity of the different states of Christendom are represented by some one of their princes ranked among the Saints; among others, the Germans by St. Henry, the English by St. Edward, the French by St. Louis, the Spaniards by St. Ferdinand, and those of the Eastern provinces by St. Helen: they give thanks to God that they have happily triumphed, by Jesus Christ, over the love of the honors and pomps of the world. Opposite are placed the penitents and anchorets who overcame its pleasures; we mark at their head St. Mary Magdalene, St. Antony, patriarch of the Cenobites, St. Jerome, St. Mary of Egypt, St. William of Maleval, founder of the Wilhelmites: and thus ends the picture of the Church in Heaven.

„That upon earth is also represented by some one personage of each of the different ecclesiastical orders, religious or political, of which she is formed: after the Sovereign Pontiff we see cardinals, prelates, priests, monks, and nuns of all the orders; and, in the second rank, the Emperor of Germany; Louis XIV, in his youth; his mother, Anne of Austria; and a multitude of persons of all conditions and countries, on whose countenances the most lively and touching expressions of piety are visible.

„Lastly, the members of the suffering Church implore the Eternal Father to shorten their torments, for the sake of the Victim Who offers Himself for them; and at the foot of the picture is this inscription, in which the whole is condensed: The most august sacrifice of the Mass, offered to God for all His intentions and for all the intentions of the Church in Heaven, on earth, and in Purgatory."

So far the account of this wonderful design; and we hope that some will be moved by it to look at the picture itself, or at the engraving in his book. It will help them to pray more fervently that they may never lose an opportunity of assisting at Mass; it will make them envy the rich, whose privilege it is to build churches and educate priests, in order that the holy sacrifice may be offered on many altars for the living and the dead. If they are priests, they will desire to preach unceasingly upon the Mass. If they are poor, they will learn to imitate so many of whom we have seen, renouncing situations because they could not hear Mass, or coming fasting till four in the afternoon, that they might receive the holy Communion.

A few years ago, the Confraternity of St. Patrick was founded at the Oratory in London for the purpose of encouraging the faithful to hear

Mass; and Pius IX, ever anxious to spread devotion among his children, granted to the members an indulgence of seven years and seven quarantines, so often as they shall induce anyone to hear Mass, and a plenary indulgence if, complying with the usual conditions of Confession and Communion, they pray according to the intention of the Holy Father on the feasts of Our Lord and of His Blessed Mother, of St. Joseph and of his patronage; of SS. Peter and Paul, St. John the Baptist, St. Patrick, St. Philip Neri, and of Blessed Sebastian Valfre. These indulgences are applicable to the Holy Souls in Purgatory. May this little book bring to many hearts a feeling of gratitude to our dear Lord for the love which He has displayed in allowing us to hear Mass, and may it move us to claim every day the grace of being present at this adorable Sacrifice.

The Immaculate Conception by Bartolome Esteban Murillo, c. 1662

Note to the Reader

Treasures, however great and precious, are never appreciated until examined, counted over, and summed up. Hence it is, dear reader, that by many there is formed no due estimate of the holy and awful sacrifice of the Mass. Though the greatest treasure which glorifies and enriches the Church of God, it is still a hidden treasure, and known to few. Ah, if this jewel of paradise were but known, who would not give up all things to obtain it! No one would then permit to escape from his mouth the scandalous words, „A Mass more or less makes little difference." Rather, like the merchant in the Gospel, would each man sink his whole fortune to render himself master of a treasure so precious: *Albiit, et vendidit omnia quoe habuit, et emit earn*, „he went and sold all that he possessed, and bought it" (St. Matt. xiii. 46).

To enlighten, therefore, him that liveth in darkness and hath no due conception of this thrice-holy mystery, is the present little work composed. But if you judge it by first appearances to be something either superfluous or presumptuous ----- superfluous, there having already issued from the press so many small works which teach so systematically and beautifully how to hear holy Mass with profit, that it would seem impossible to wish for more; or presumptuous, on the ground that a far other order of talent is needed for the illustration of a mystery so venerable as to surpass the apprehension of the very seraphim ----- I must with all ingenuousness allow that you speak the truth, and confess that I have nothing to reply. Indeed, these two considerations have held me back for some time, and I have experienced no slight repugnance to a work so likely to be received as something quite unneeded, as an attempt beyond my strength ----- and, therefore, a public stain on one's credit.

Two motives have, however, afforded an impulse sufficient to overcome the obstinate reluctance of my heart. The first is an exhortation, which I have venerated as a command, from one whom, by many titles, I hold myself bound to obey. The second motive is the hope that I might extend some little aid to the people whom I have already culti-

vated by missions. One of the greatest benefits resulting from these is the increased habitual homage and veneration toward the Most Holy Sacrament. Missions excite a holy fervor, spurring on the hearers to seek more frequent nourishment from the Bread of Angels, and to escort the most holy Viaticum whenever it is borne to the sick, so that it may be beheld accompanied by crowds of people and by multitudes of lights; in short, with all dignity, solemnity, and decorum. Still greater is the diligence used in these missions to induce all daily to hear holy Mass. Now, it cannot be easily imagined how much it assists the attainment of this holy end to place in the hands of the poor some little book composed in plain and simple style, and thus adapted to their capacity. Such books clear away difficulties in the way of devotion, affording light to the understanding and fervor to the heart, and not seldom bring about greater gain than all the efforts of preachers. Our poor words take flight and are gone, while written exhortations remain before the eye. Were this little work thus to turn out an aid to but one single soul, it could not be called quite superfluous.

In order that it may become more profitable to the unlearned, it shall be divided under three distinct heads. In the first place, there shall be set forth a short instruction upon the excellence of, and necessity for, holy Mass. In the second, there shall be taught a practical and devout method of hearing it with profit. In the third, there shall be narrated some examples, which may act upon the hearts of persons of every condition, as stimulants to the hearing of it daily.

Such, then, are the motives which should excite in you some sympathy for me, if the attempt still appear too ambitious, and which awaken in me the hope of being useful even to you, who, perhaps, are not very complacent toward it, because, before the close, I shall reveal to you a hidden treasure which, if you but know how to avail yourselves of it, will enrich you with all good in life and in death, in time and in eternity. Farewell, and may all blessings attend you.

The Mass of St. Gregory by Petrus Moraulus, c. 1530

Chapter 1

The Three Excellenceies of Mass
Part 1.

I.

I requires great patience to endure the language of careless livers, breathing atheism itself, and ruinous to devotion; as for instance, „A Mass more or less counts for little." „It is no small thing to hear Mass on festivals." „The Mass of this or that priest is for length like one in Holy Week; when he appears at the altar, I generally get out of church forthwith." He who talks in this way lets it be perceived that he has little or no esteem for the thrice-holy sacrifice af the Mass. That sacrifice is the sun of Christianity, the soul of faith, the centre of the Catholic religion, wherein are beheld all her rites, all her ceremonies, and all her Sacraments; in fine, it is the compendium of all the good and beautiful to be found in the Church of God. Wherefore, O ye who now read my words, ponder well how great are the matters to be spoken of in these instructions.

II.

It is a certain truth that all the religions which have existed from the beginning of the world have ever had some sacrifice as an essential part of the worship which they offered to God. But because their whole law was either vain or imperfect, so were their sacrifices either vain or imperfect. Most vain were the sacrifices of the idolaters, nor is there any occasion to mention them; and those of the Hebrews, although, indeed, then professing the true religion, were poor and deficient, by St. Paul called *infirma et egena elementa*, „weak and poor elements" (Gal. iv. 9), because they could neither cancel sin nor confer grace. The sole sacrifice which we have in our holy religion, that is to say,

Holy Mass, is a sacrifice, holy, perfect, in every point complete, with which each one of the faithful nobly honors God, protesting at one and the same time his own nothingness and the supreme dominion which God hath over him; a sacrifice called, therefore, by David, *sacrificium justitiae*, „the sacrifice of justice" (Ps. iv. 5); both because it contains the Just One Himself, and the Saint of Saints, or rather justice and holiness themselves, and because it sanctifies souls by the infusion of grace and the affluence of gifts which it confers. Being, then, a sacrifice so holy ----- a sacrifice the most venerable and the most excellent of all ----- in order that you may form a due conception of so great a treasure, we shall here explain, in a manner quite succinct, some of its Divine excellencies. To express them all were not a work to which our poor faculties could attain.

III.

The principal excellence of the most Holy Sacrifice of the Mass consists in being essentially, and in the very highest degree, identical with that which was offered on the Cross of Calvary: with this sole difference, that the Sacrifice on the Cross was bloody, and made once for all, and did on that one occasion satisfy fully for all the sins of the world; while the Sacrifice of the Altar is an unbloody sacrifice, which can be repeated an infinite number of times, and was instituted in order to apply in detail that universal ransom which Jesus paid for us on Calvary. So that the bloody Sacrifice was the instrument of redemption; the unbloody is that which puts us in possession: the one threw open the treasury of the merits of Christ Our Lord; the other affords the practical use of that treasury. And, therefore, observe that in Mass there is made not a mere representation, nor a simple commemoration of the Passion and Death of the Redeemer, but there is performed, in a certain true sense, the selfsame most holy act which was performed on Calvary. It may be said, with all truth, that in every Mass Our Redeemer returns mystically to die for us, without really dying, at one and the same time really alive and as it were slain ----- *vidi Agnum stantem tamquam occisum*, „I saw a Lamb standing as it were slain" (Apoc. v. 6). On the anniversary day of the holy Nativity there is represented by the Church the birth of the Lord, but Our Lord is not then born. On the day of the Ascension and on the day of Pentecost, there are shadowed forth the ascent of the Lord to Heaven, and the coming of the Holy Spirit down to the earth; yet it is by no means true that, as each of these days comes round, the Lord again ascends to Heaven, or the Holy Spirit visibly descends to earth. But the same cannot be said of the mystery of Holy Mass, for in it there is made no simple representation of a bygone event, but the selfsame Sacrifice is unbloodily made which, with the shedding of Blood, was made upon the Cross. That same Body, that same Blood, that same Jesus Who then offered Himself upon Calvary, now offers Himself in the Holy Mass. *Opus*, says the Church, *opus nostrae redemptionis exercetur* (Orat. s. in Mis. Dom. 9, post Pent). Yes; *exercetur*; in Mass there is effected, there is continuously practised, that same Sacrifice which was made upon the Cross. Oh, awful, solemn, and stupendous work!

Now, tell me whether, when you enter church to hear Mass, you thoroughly well consider that you are going up as it were to Calvary, to be present at the death of the Redeemer. If so, would you go with behavior so unsubdued, with dress so flaunting? If the Magdalene had gone to Calvary, to the foot of the Cross, all dressed out, perfumed, and adorned, as when she associated with her lovers, what would have been said of her? What, then, shall be said of you who go to holy Mass as if you were going to a ball? But what shall be said if you profane those functions of most dread sanctity with nods and becks, with tattle, with laughter, with the petty attentions of courtship, or with graver sacrileges of thought, word, or deed? Wickedness is hideous at any time, and in any place; but sins committed during the time of Mass, and before the altar, draw down after them the curse of God. *Maledictus homo qui tacit opus Domini fraudulenter* (Jer. xlviii. 10). Think seriously upon this, while I proceed to disclose to you yet other marvels and glories of this all-precious treasure.

IV.

It seems to me impossible for a religious function to possess a prerogative more excellent than this of the Holy Sacrifice of Mass, that it is no mere copy, but one original with the Sacrifice of the Cross. Still further is its eminence enhanced by having for its priest none else than God made man. In so great a sacrifice three things attract consideration: the priest who offers, the Victim offered, and the majesty of Him to Whom the offering is made. Now observe the marvellous grandeur of Holy Mass, in virtue of each of these three considerations. The Priest Who offers is the Man-God Christ Jesus; the Victim is the Life of God; nor is it offered to any other than unto God. Rekindle, then, your faith, and recognize the true celebrant to be not so much the human priest as the adorable person of Our Lord Jesus Christ. He is the primary offerer, not only because He has instituted this Holy Sacrifice, and has given to it all its efficacy through His merits, but also because in each Mass He Himself deigns for our good to, transubstantiate the bread and wine into His most Holy Body and into His most Precious Blood. Behold, then, the chiefest privilege of Holy Mass, to have for priest God made man; and when you see the celebrant at the altar, know that his highest dignity consists in being the minister of that invisible and eternal Priest, Our Redeemer Himself. Hence it results that the sacrifice itself does not cease to be agreeable to God, although the priest who celebrates may be wicked and sacrilegious, seeing that the principal offerer is Christ Our Lord, and the priest is His mere minister. In the same way, anyone who gives alms by the hand of a servant is called in all truth the giver; and even though his servant may be wicked and infamous, yet if the master be good, the alms do not cease to be praiseworthy and holy. Blessed, then, be God, Who hath bestowed on us a holy, a most holy Priest, Who offers to the Eternal Father this Divine Sacrifice, not only in every place (the holy faith being now everywhere diffused), but every day, and even every hour; since the sun is rising to others, while to us it sets. At every hour, then, in various parts of the world, this most perfectly holy Priest offers to the Father His Blood, His Soul, and His whole self for us: and all this He does as many times as there are Masses celebrated in the whole world. O boundless treasure! O mine of inestimable stores thus possessed by us in the Church of God! O happy we if we could but assist at all these Masses! What a store of reward would be thus acquired! What a heaping up of graces in this life, what a fund of glory in the other, would be the fruit of so loving an attendance!

V.

But what is implied in this word „attendance?" Those who hear Mass not only perform the office of attendants, but likewise of offerers, having themselves a right to the title of priests. *Fecisti nos Deo nostro regnum et sacerdotes* (Apoc. v. 10). The celebrating priest is, as it were, the public minister of the Church in general; he is the intermediary between all the faithful, particularly those who assist at Mass, and the invisible Priest, Who is Christ; and, together with Christ, he offers to the Eternal Father, both in behalf of all the rest and of himself, the great price of human redemption. But he is not alone in this so holy function, since all those who assist at Mass concur with him in offering the sacrifice; and, therefore, the priest turns round to the people and says, *Orate fratres ut meum ac vestrum sacrificium acceptabile fiat* ----- „Pray, O my brethren, that mine and your sacrifice may be acceptable to God;" in order that the faithful may understand that, while he indeed acts the part of principal minister, all those who are present make the great offering together with him. So that when you assist at Holy Mass, you perform, after a certain manner, the office of priest. What say you, then? Will you ever dare, from this time forward, to be at Mass sitting, prating, looking here and there, perhaps even sleeping, or content yourselves with reciting some vocal prayers, without at all taking to heart the tremendous office of priest which you are exercising? Ah me! I cannot restrain myself from exclaiming, O dull and incapable world, that understandest nothing of mysteries so sublime! How is it possible that anyone should remain before the altar with a mind distracted and a heart dissipated at a time when the holy Angels stand there trembling and astonished at the contemplation of a work so stupendous?

VI.

You are surprised, perhaps, to hear me speak of the Mass as a stupendous work. But what tongue, human or angelic, may ever describe a power so immeasurable as that exercised by the simplest priest in Mass? And who could ever have imagined that the voice of man, which by nature hath not the power even to raise a straw from the ground, should obtain through grace a power so stupendous as to bring from Heaven to earth the Son of God? It is a greater power than that which would be required to change the place of mountains, to dry up seas, and to turn round the heavens; it even emulates, in a certain manner, that first *fiat* with which God brought all things out of nothing, and in some sort would seem to surpass that other *fiat* with which the sweet Virgin drew down into her bosom the Eternal Word. She did nothing else than supply matter for the body of Christ ----- made indeed *from* her and her most pure blood, but not *by* her, in the sense of her own potential act. But altogether different, and most marvellous, is the sacramental manner in which the voice of the priest, operating as the instrument of Christ, reproduces Him, and does so as often as he consecrates. The Blessed Giovanni Buono made this truth (S. Ant. 3 p. hist. tit. 24, c. 13) in some sort comprehensible to a hermit, his companion, who was unable to imagine how the words of a priest could be allowed such power as to change the substance of bread into the Body of Jesus Christ, and the substance of wine into His Blood, and who, unhappily, had consented to the devilish suggestions of doubt. The good servant of God, perceiving this man's error, conducted him to a fountain, took thence a cup of water, and gave it him to drink. He, when he had drunk of it, declared that during his whole life he had never tasted a wine so pleasant. Then Giovanni Buono said, „Do not you now feel, my dear brother, the marvellous truth? If, through means of me, a miserable man, water is changed into wine by Divine power, how much more ought you to believe that, through means of the words of God ----- for the priest only uses the words instituted for the purpose by God Himself ----- the bread and wine are converted into the substance of the Body and Blood of Christ? Who shall dare to assign limits to the omnipotence of God?" This so effectually enlightened the hermit that, banishing every doubt from his mind, he did great penance for his sin. Let us have but a little faith, a little living faith, and we shall confess that the mighty and admirable things contained in this adorable sacrifice are without number; nor will it then seem too strange to us to behold the marvel repeated continually ----- the thrice-holy humanity of Jesus multiplying itself in thousands and thousands of places, enjoying, so to speak, a kind of infinity denied to every other body, and reserved to it alone through the merit of His life, sacrificed to the Most

High. It is said to have been once granted to an unbelieving Jew to have the mystery of this multiplied existence illustrated by the mouth of a woman. He was amusing himself in the public square, when there passed a priest who, accompanied by a crowd, carried the most holy Viaticum to a sick person. All the people, bending the knee, rendered due homage of adoration to the Most Holy Sacrament; the Jew alone made no movement, nor gave any token of reverence. This being seen by a poor woman, she exclaimed, „O miserable man, why do you not show reverence to the true God, present in this Divine Sacrament?" „What true God?" said the Jew, sharply. „If this were so, would not there be many Gods, since on each of your altars there is one during Mass?" The woman instantly took a sieve, and holding it up to the sun, told the Jew to look at the rays which passed through the chinks; and then added, „Tell me, Jew, are there many suns which pass through the openings of this sieve, or only one?" And the Jew answering that there was but one sun. „Then," replied the woman, „why do you wonder that God incarnate, veiled in the Sacrament, though one, indivisible, and unchanged, should, through excess of love, place Himself in true and Real Presence on different altars?" Through this illustration, he was held on to confess the truth of the faith. O holy faith! A ray of thy light is needed in order to reply with energy of spirit to the captiousness of carnal minds. Yes, who shall ever dare to assign limits to the omnipotence of God? Through the great conception which St. Teresa had of the omnipotence of God, she was wont to say that the more lofty, deep, and abstruse to our understandings are the mysteries of our holy faith, with so much the more firmness, and with so much the greater devotion, did she believe them; knowing full well that the Almighty God could work prodigies infinitely greater still. Revive, then, your faith with heavenly grace, and, acknowledging this divine sacrifice to be the miracle of miracles, feelingly confess that majesty so great must needs be incomprehensible to our poor minds, and is, therefore, the more sublime; then, full of astonishment, exclaim again and yet again, „O treasure, how great! treasure of O love, how immense!"

The Three Excellenceies of Mass
Part 2.

VII.

*B*ut if the intrinsic wonder and glory of the sacrifice move you not, be moved at least by the extreme necessity for its existence.

If there were no sun to shine on the world, what would it be? All darkness, horror, barrenness, and misery supreme. And if there were not holy Mass in the world? O unhappy race! We should then be vessels empty of every good, and full of evil to the brim; we should be a mark for all the thunders of the wrath of God. Some are surprised at its really seeming as if since ancient times our good God had in some sort changed His mode of government. He then caused Himself to be called the God of armies and of battles, and spoke to the people from the midst of clouds, with lightnings in His hand. He then chastised sin with all the rigor of justice. For one adultery there fell by the edge of the sword five-and-twenty thousand of the tribe of Benjamin. For the pride of David in numbering the people He sent a pestilence so malignant that quickly seventy thousand persons were no more. For one curious and somewhat irreverent look He overthrew in frightful slaughter more than fifty thousand of the Betsamites. And now He will bear with patience not only vanities and frivolities, but adulteries the most base, scandals the most iniquitous, and blasphemies the most revolting, vomited forth against His most holy name by many Christians every hour of the day. How comes this? Why so great a difference of government? Are, perhaps, our sins of ingratitude more excusable than those of old? Quite the contrary. They are very much more culpable, since there is the addition of benefits so immeasurable. The true reason of a clemency so stupendous is the holy Mass, in which is offered to the Eternal Father the great Victim-Jesus. Behold the Sun of holy Church, that scatters the clouds and renders heaven again serene! Behold the heavenly Rainbow, pacifying the storms of Divine justice!

For myself, I believe that were it not for holy Mass, at this moment the world would be in the abyss, unable to bear up under the mighty load of its iniquities. Mass is the potent prop that holds the world upon its base. Therefore, when we are assisting at it, we ought to practise that which once Alphonsus of Albuquerque did, who, finding himself with his fleet in danger of perishing during a fierce and terrific tempest, adopted the following means: He took in his arms an innocent little child which was on board his ship, and lifting it up toward Heaven, he said, „If we are sinners, this creature is certainly free from sin; O Lord, for love of this innocent, remit to us the death we deserve!" Will you believe it? The spectacle of that stainless babe was so pleasing to God that He tranquillized the sea, and changed into joy for these unfortunates their terror of a death already imminent. Now, what do you believe is done by the Eternal Father when the priest, lifting in the air the thrice-saved Victim, shows to Him the innocence of His Divine Son? Ah, then His compassion cannot resist the sight of the most spotless innocence of Jesus, and He feels as if compelled to calm our storms, and to provide for all our necessities. Thus without that thrice-holy Victim, Jesus, first of all bloodily sacrificed for us upon the Cross, and daily since unbloodily upon our altars, it would be all at an end with us; each might say to the other, „We part to meet in Hell." Yes, in Hell! But possessing this treasure of holy Mass, hope breathes again; and if we but throw it not away by our own mismanagement, we have holy Paradise within our grasp. Well may we, therefore, kiss our altars, perfume them with incense and holy sweets; and, what is more, honor them with the utmost reverence and awe, since through them there cometh so much good. And do you, O priests, join your hands in thanksgiving to the Eternal Father for having placed you in the sweet necessity of often offering to Him this Victim of paradise; and, still more, thank Him for the unbounded gain which you can gather from it, if you but be faithful, not only in offering it, but in offering it for the proper ends for which He bestowed a gift so precious.

VIII.

A sense of what is noble and virtuous does undoubtedly supply very powerful influences whereby to move the human heart; but a perception of what averts calamity, or secures an advantage, is generally still more powerful. Should, then, the glory and the beauty of the holy sacrifice be of small importance in your eyes, how shall you fail to appreciate the vast gain it brings to both good and wicked, both during life and at the hour of death, nay, even after death itself? Imagine yourself to be that debtor in the Gospel who, burdened with the heavy debt of ten thousand talents, and summoned to account, humbled himself, pleading and beseeching time fully to satisfy his obligations ----- *Patientiam habe in me, et omnia reddam tibi*, „Have patience with me, and I will pay thee all" (St. Matt. xviii. 26). The very same should you do, for you have not one but many debts with the bank of Divine justice. You should humble yourself, and solicit so much time as is needed for hearing holy Mass; and be sure that thus it is possible for you most fully to satisfy for all. The angelic St. Thomas (1. ii., art. 3, ed. 19) suggests what those obligations are which we all owe to God, saying that they are specially four, and that each of the four is infinite. The first is, to praise and honor His infinite Majesty, worthy of infinite honor, infinite praise. The second is, to satisfy for so many sins committed against that infinite Majesty. The third is, to thank Him for so many benefits received. The fourth is, to supplicate Him as the Giver of all graces. Now, how shall we wretched creatures, who are in a state of dependence for the very breath we draw, ever be able to fulfiLl obligations such as these? Behold the method, a method most sweet and easy, which should console me, which should console you, and every one? Let us take care to attend many Masses, to attend with all the devotion possible, and to cause them to be celebrated elsewhere as frequently as we can; and thus, were our debts the most exorbitant, were they even literally innumerable, there is no room to doubt but that with this treasure we might be able most fully to pay them all. But, in order that you may have a fuller perception of these your debts, we shall explain the four classes of them, one by one; and you will then find no small consolation in viewing the inexhaustible means which you possess for their payment in the rich mine of the holy sacrifice.

IX.

The first obligation by which we are bound toward God is to honor

Him. It is indeed a precept of the natural law itself that every inferior owes homage to his superior, and by so much the higher the superiority, so much the deeper the homage that should be offered. Whence it results that, as Almighty God possesses a greatness utterly unbounded, there is due to Him an unbounded honor. Oh, wretched that we are! Where, where shall we ever find an offering worthy of our Creator? Turn your eyes round among all the creatures of the universe ----- no, you will not find one that is worthy of God. Ah, no! an offering worthy of God can be none other than God Himself. And He Who resides on the throne of His greatness, He it is that must needs descend to lay Himself a Victim on our altars, in order that the homage rendered may perfectly correspond to the eminence of that infinite Majesty. This it is which is effected in holy Mass. In it Almighty God is honored as He deserves, because He is honored by that God Himself, that is to say, by Jesus, Who, placing Himself in character of Victim on the altar, with an act of inexplicable submission, adores the Most Holy Trinity, even as it is adorable ----- in such manner that all other acts of homage, by all other beings, vanish before the face of this self-humiliation of Jesus, as stars before the sun. It is told of a holy soul (*Sanct. Jure.* p. 3, c. 10) that, enamored of God, the fire of her charity flashed forth in a thousand longings. „O my God," she said, „my God, would that I had as many hearts, as many tongues as there are leaves on the trees, atoms of the air, and drops in the waters, that I might so love Thee, and so honor Thee, as Thou deservest! Oh, had I but in this hand all creatures, I would place them at Thy feet, so that all might melt themselves away in love before Thee; and then, oh, that I might but love Thee more than all of them united ----- yes, more than all the Angels, more than all the Saints, more than all Paradise itself!" One day when she had done this with the utmost fervor, she heard herself thus answered by Our Lord: „Console thyself, my daughter; by one Mass heard with devotion thou wilt render to Me all that glory which thou desirest, and infinitely more." You wonder, perhaps, at this, but you are wrong; for our good Jesus, being not only man, but omnipotent God, by humiliating Himself on the altar, offers in that act of humiliation to the Most Holy Trinity homage and honor infinite; so that we who join with Him in offering the great sacrifice attain ----- yes, even we, through Him ----- to the privilege of rendering an infinite homage and honor unto

God. Oh, how great a thought! Let us repeat it yet once again, since it so much imports us to know it: We ----- yes, even we ----- by attending holy Mass, may render to God homage and honor infinite. Be now confounded for very wonder, reflecting that the proposition just laid down is indeed most true; a soul assisting with adequate devotion at holy Mass renders more honor to God than that which all the Angels and all the Saints put together render with all their adorations. For, after all, they also are but mere creatures, and their homage is therefore limited and finite; whereas, in Mass, Jesus humbles Himself, a humiliation of infinite merit and value; and thus the homage and honor which we through Him give to God in Mass is an homage and honor infinite. And oh, what blessedness, if it is really so, that through a devout hearing of holy Mass this our obligation is fulfilled! O blinded world, when will you open your eyes to understand truths which so much concern you? And you have yet the heart to say, „A Mass more or less matters little!" O mournful, dreadful blindness!

X.

The second obligation by which we are bound toward God is to satisfy His justice for the commission of so many sins. Oh, what a measureless debt is this! One single mortal sin so weighs in the scales of Divine justice, that to satisfy for it, all the good works of all the Martyrs and of all the Saints who as yet have existed, who exist now, or ever shall exist, would not suffice. And, yet, with the holy sacrifice of the Mass, viewed according to its intrinsic preciousness and value, satisfaction may be completely made for all committed sin: and that you may understand how much you are thus obliged to Jesus, attend to what I now say. Although truly He is the very party offended, yet, not contented with having satisfied Divine justice for us on Calvary, He hath bestowed, and doth continuously bestow, on us this method of satisfaction in the holy sacrifice of Mass; for, as there is renewed in Mass the offering which Jesus hath already made on the Cross to the Eternal Father for the sins of the whole world, that same Divine blood which was once paid down as the general ransom of the whole human race comes to be specially applied to each of us individually, by being offered in Mass for the sins of him who celebrates, and of all those who assist at so tremendous a sacrifice. Not that the sacrifice of Mass by any means cancels our sins immediately, and of itself, as does the Sacrament of Penance: but it cancels them mediately, calling down various aids of interior impulse, of holy aspiration, and of actual grace, all tending toward a worthy repentance of our sins, either at the time of Mass itself or at some other fitting time.

Therefore, God alone knows how many souls issue from the filth of sins through the extraordinary aids which come to them by this Divine sacrifice. And here reflect that although indeed the man in mortal sin is not aided by the sacrifice as a propitiation, it yet avails as supplication; and therefore all sinners ought to hear many Masses, in order to obtain more easily the grace of conversion. To souls that live in grace it gives a wonderful force, tending to maintain them in their happy state, while it immediately cancels (according to the most common view) the guilt of all venial sins, provided, at least, that as a whole they are repented of, according to what St. Augustine clearly says: *Si quis devote audiat Missam, non incidet in peccatum mortale, et venialia remittentur ei (Sup. Can. Quia passus, de Consecr. dist. 2)*, „He who devoutly hears holy Mass will receive a great vigor to enable him to resist mortal sin, and there shall be pardoned to him all venial sins which he may have committed up to that hour." Nor should this surprise; for if, as St. Gregory narrates (Dial 1. 4, c. 57), the Masses which a poor woman caused to be celebrated every Monday for the soul of her husband, who had been enslaved by barbarians and was thought by her to be dead, caused the chains to be loosened from his feet, and the manacles from his arms, so that ever while these Masses were being celebrated he remained free and unchained, as he himself declared on his return; how much more must not we believe such a sacrifice to be most efficacious for the loosening of spiritual bonds, such as venial sins, bonds which hold the soul, as it were, imprisoned, leaving it no power to work with that freedom and fervor with which it would work were it not for these impediments? O blessed Mass, setting at liberty the sons of God, and satisfying all the penalties due to so many offences!

XI.

You will, perhaps, say to me, it suffices, then, to hear one single Mass to strike off the heaviest debts due to God through many committed sins, because, Mass being of infinite value, we can therewith pay to God an infinite satisfaction. Not so fast, by your leave; because, though indeed Mass is of infinite value, you must know, nevertheless, that Almighty God accepts it in a manner limited and finite, and in degrees conformable to the greater or less perfection in the dispositions of him who celebrates or who assists at the sacrifice. *Quorum tibi fides cognita est, et nota devotio,* says holy Church, in the Canon of Mass, suggesting by this method of speech that which the great teachers expressly lay down (*De Lug.* dist. 9, n. 103); namely, that the grater or less satisfaction applied in our behalf by the sacrifice becomes determined by the higher or lower dispositions of the celebrant, or of the assistants, as just now mentioned. Now, then, consider the spiritual bewilderment of those who go in search of the quickest and least devoutly conducted Masses, and, what is worse, assist at them with little or no devotion; nor have any zeal in causing them to be celebrated, or in selecting with that view the more fervent and devout of the priesthood. It is true, according to St. Thomas (3 p. quo 82, art. 6), that all the sacrifices are, as Sacraments, equal in rank; but they are not, therefore, equal in the effects resulting from them; whence the greater the actual or habitual piety of the celebrant, so much the greater will be the fruit of the application of the Mass; so that not to recognize the difference between a tepid and devout priest, in respect to the efficacy of his Mass, will be simply not to heed whether the net with which you fish be small or great. [Emphasis added here and below.] The same reasoning applies in regard to those attending Mass. And, truly, while I exhort you, to the best of my knowledge and power, to attend many Masses, I yet admonish you to have far more regard to devotion in hearing than to the number heard; because, if you shall have more devotion in one single Mass than another man in fifty, you will give more honor to God in that single Mass, and you will extract from it greater fruit, in the way called ex opere operato, than that other with all his fifty. *In satisfactione*, says St. Thomas, *magis attenditur affectus offerentis quam quantitas obiationis* (3 p. quo 79, art. 5). It is true, indeed, (as a grave author asserts,) that through one single Mass, attended with singularly perfect devotion, it might possibly happen that the justice of God would remain satisfied for all the transgressions of some great sinner. And this is quite in harmony with what the holy Council of Trent teaches; namely, that by the offering of this holy sacrifice God grants the gift of penitence, and then by means of true penitence pardons sins the most grave and enormous. *Hujus quippe oblatione gratiam et donum paenitentiae concedens crimina et peccata etiam ingentia dimittit* (Sess. xxii. cap. 2). Yet notwithstanding all this, since neither the internal dispositions with which you attend Mass are manifest to yourself, nor the amount of satisfaction which corresponds thereto, you should make sure to the best of your power by attending many Masses, and by attending with all the devotion possible. Blessed are you if you maintain a great confidence in the loving mercy of God, which shines so wonderfully forth in this Divine sacrifice; and with lively faith and devout recollection attend as many Masses as you can; for I declare that, doing this with perseverance, you may attain to the sweet hope of reaching Heaven without any intervening share in Purgatory. To Mass, then, dearest friends, and never allow yourselves to utter the thought, „A Mass more or less is of little consequence."

XII.

The third obligation is that of gratitude for the immense benefits which our most loving God hath bestowed upon us. Put in one heap all the gifts, all the graces you have received from God ----- so many gifts of nature and of grace, body, soul, senses, and faculties, and health, and life itself; yes, the very life, too, of His Son Jesus, and His death suffered for us, which in themselves immeasurably swell the great debt which we owe to God ----- and how shall we ever be able sufficiently to thank Him? On the one hand, the law of gratitude is observed by the very beasts, who sometimes change their cruel anger into gentle homage to their benefactors; and how much more, of course, has it not to be observed by man, gifted as he is with reason, and so nobly endowed by the Divine liberality! But, on the other hand, our poverty is so great that there is no way of truly making any return for all the blessings of God; because the least of them all, coming as it does from the hands of majesty so divine, and accompanied as it is by an infinite love on His part, thus acquires an infinite value, and lays us under a debt of infinite correspondence in the way of reverence and love. O poor, miserable things that we are! If we are incapable of sustaining the weight of one single benefit, how shall we ever be able to bear the burden of so many, so countlessly many? Then, here we are, placed in the hard necessity of living and dying, as it were, ungrateful to our Supreme Benefactor. But no: take heart; the way most fully to thank our good God is taught us by holy David, who, led by Divine inspiration to speak with mysterious reference to this Divine sacrifice, indicates that nothing can sufficiently render the thanks which are due to God, excepting holy Mass. *Quid retribuam Domino pro omnibus quae retribuit mihi?* „What return shall I offer to the Lord for all the benefits which He hath bestowed upon me?" And answering himself, he says, *Calicern salutaris accipiam*; or, according to another version, *Calicem levabo* ----- „I will uplift on high the chalice of the Lord;" that is, I will offer a sacrifice most grateful to Him, and with this alone I shall satisfy the debt of so many and such signal benefits. Add to this that the sacrifice was instituted by Our Redeemer principally in recognition of the Divine beneficence, and as thanks to Him; and therefore it bears as its most special and worthy name the Eucharist, which signifies an Offering of Thanks. He Himself also gave us the example when, in the Last Supper, before the act of Consecration in that first Mass, He raised His eyes to Heaven, and gave thanks to His heavenly Father: *Elevatis oculis in caelum, Tibi gratias agens fregit.* O Divine thanksgiving, disclosing the chief end for which was instituted this tremendous sacrifice, and which invites us to conform ourselves to the example of our Head, so that in every Mass at which we assist we may know how to avail ourselves of so great a treasure, and offer it in gratitude to our Supreme Benefactor! And all the more, since the beloved Virgin, and the Angels, and the Saints, rejoice to witness this our tribute of thanks to so great a King.

XIII.

The life of the venerable Sister Francesca Farnese was at one time troubled by a thousand anxieties of heavenly love. She mourned to see herself covered from head to foot with Divine benefits, and yet unable to prove in act the gratitude she felt, by making to her Lord any competent return. Behold, one day there is said to have appeared to her the most holy Virgin, who put into her arms her heavenly Babe. „Take Him," she said, „for He is yours, and because with Him alone you will fulfill all your duties." O blessed Mass, by which we come to have the Son of God placed, not only within our arms, but in our hearts. *Parvulus datus est nobis.* Nor is there a doubt but that with Him, and Him alone, we shall be able to satisfy the debt of gratitude which we have contracted with God. We almost seem in Mass to render to God more than He has given to us ----- not in reality, of course, but in appearance, since once only hath the Eternal Father given to us His Divine Son in His Incarnation, while we give Him back to Him again innumerable times in this holy sacrifice. Thus we seem to have the advantage, not in the quality of the gift ----- it being impossible for greater to be given than the Son of God ----- but apparently by the repetition so many times of that self-same gift. Truly, He gives it to us each time, for us to offer back again; but, at any rate, there it is, an infinite offering on our part, offered many times. O great God! O most loving God! Oh, for tongues infinite in number and power, to give Thee infinite thanks for so great a treasure! If, reader, in time past it has lain hidden from you, now that you begin to know it, can you fail to exclaim, „Oh, the treasure bestowed upon me! how great ----- how great thou art!"

XIV.

But the immense benefit of the holy sacrifice of Mass does not end here. It is in our power by means of it to pay the fourth debt due to God, which is to supplicate Him, and to entreat new graces of Him. Try to realize to yourself how great are your miseries both of body and of soul, and the need, therefore, in which you are of having recourse to God, in order that at every moment He may assist and succor you, for assuredly He alone is the end and the beginning of all your good, whether temporal or eternal. On the other hand, what courage, what heart have you for asking new benefits, seeing the utter ingratitude with which you have failed to respond to so many favors already bestowed on you ----- nay, seeing you have even turned into offences against Him the very graces He gave you? But still take courage, take heart. If you do not deserve new benefits, your good Jesus has deserved them for you. He has desired for this end to be for you in Mass a pacifying Victim, a supplicatory sacrifice, for obtaining from the Father everything of which you have need. Yes, yes: in holy Mass our dear beloved Jesus, as the chief and supreme Priest, recommends our cause to the Father, prays for us, and makes Himself our advocate. If we knew on some occasion that the great and blessed Virgin was uniting herself with us in prayer to the Eternal Father to obtain for us the graces we desired, what confidence should we not conceive of being heard? What hope, then, what confidence should we not have, knowing that in Mass Jesus Himself prays for us, offers His most precious blood to the Eternal Father for us, and makes Himself our advocate! O blessed Mass! O mine of all our good!

XV.

But let us dig farther into the depth of this mine, in order to discover more of the vast treasures contained in it. Oh, what precious gems lie there! What graces, virtues, and gifts holy Mass calls down! In the first place, it calls down all spiritual graces, all the goods appertaining to the soul, such as repentance for sins, and victory over temptations, whether such result from external trials, as bad companions and infernal spirits, or internal, as for instance, those arising from rebellious appetites. It calls down the aid of grace, so necessary for enabling us to rise up, to stand upon our feet, to walk forward in the ways of God. It calls down many good and holy inspirations, and many internal impulses, which dispose us to shake off tepidity, and spurs us on to work our best with greater fervor, with will more prompt, with intention more upright and pure; and these, again, bring with them an inestimable treasure, being the most effectual means for obtaining from God the grace of final perseverance, on which depends our eternal salvation, and the grace, of as much moral certainty of eternal bliss as is ever permitted here below. But further still, it calls down temporal blessings, so far as these may not oppose the salvation of the soul, such as health, abundance, peace, with the exclusion of the evils which are their opposites, such as pestilences, earthquakes, wars, famines, persecutions, hatreds, calumnies, injuries; in fine, here may we find liberation from all evils, here may we find enrichment by every sort of benefit. In a word, holy Mass is the golden key of Paradise; and while the Eternal Father gives us this key, which of all His other benefits can He refuse? *Qui proprio suo Filio non pepercit*, says St. Paul, *sed pro nobis omnibus tradidit ilium, quomodo non etiam cum ilio omnia nobis donavit?* „He that: spared not even His Own Son, but delivered Him up for us; all, how hath He not also, with Him, given us all things?" (Rom. viii. 32.) Now, was not that good priest quite right who used to say that whatever he asked of God, even the loftiest height of grace, for himself or others, while celebrating holy Mass, he seemed to himself to be asking, nothing in comparison with the offering which he was engaged in making to Him? (Osor. Com. 8, tom. 4.) He reasoned thus: All the favors which I ask of God in Mass are finite, whereas the gift which I offer to Him is uncreated and infinite, and so, the account being rightly summed, I am the creditor, He the debtor. The good priest by no means purposed to deny that the power of offering the gift, and the gift itself, came first from God; but, putting it thus, he courageously besought great graces, and received yet greater. And you ----- why do not you also awake? Why not demand great graces? Take my advice, and in every Mass ask God to make you a great Saint. Does this seem too much? It is not too much. Is it not our good Master Who protests in the holy Gospel that, for a cup of cold water given out of love of Him, He will, in return, give Paradise? How, then, while offering to God the blood of His most blessed Son, should He not give you a hundred heavens, were there so many? How can you doubt but that He wishes to give you all the virtues and all the perfections which are required to make you a Saint, and a great Saint, in Heaven? O blessed Mass! Expand yet more and more your heart, and ask great things of Him, with the reflection that you ask of a God Who does not grow poor by giving, and, therefore, the more you petition for, the more you will obtain.

XVI.

But ----- will you believe it? ----- besides the benefits which we ask in holy Mass, our good God grants many others which we do not ask. St. Jerome distinctly declares, *Absque dubio dot nobis Dominus quod in Missa petimus; et quod magis est, sape dot quod non petimus* (cap. cum. mart. de celeb. Miss.). „Without doubt," says the Saint, „the Lord grants all the favors which are asked of Him in Mass, provided they be those fitting for us; and, which is a matter of greater wonder, ofttimes He grants that also which is not demanded of Him, if we, on our part, put no obstacle in the way." Whence it may be said that Mass is the sun of the human race, scattering its splendors over good and wicked; nor is there a soul so vile on earth who, hearing holy Mass, doth not carry away from it some great good, often without asking, often without even thinking of it. This is the lesson conveyed by the famous legend told by St. Antoninus of two youths, both libertines, who went one day into the forest, one of them having heard Mass, the other not. Soon, it is said, there arose a furious tempest, and they heard, amid thunder and lightning, a voice which cried „Slay!" and instantly came a flash which reduced to ashes the one who had not heard Mass. The other, all terrified, was seeking escape, when he heard anew the same voice, which repeated „Slay!" The poor youth expected instant death, when lo! he heard another voice, which answered, „I cannot, I cannot; today he heard, *Verbum caro factum est,'* His Mass will not let me strike." Oh, how many times hath God freed you from death, or at least from many most grievous perils, through the Mass which you have attended! St. Gregory assures us of this in the fourth of his dialogues: *Per auditionem Missae homo liberatur amultis malis et periculis.* „It is most true," says the holy Doctor, „that he who attends holy Mass shall be freed from many evils and from many dangers, both foreseen and unforeseen." „He shall," as St. Augustine sums it up, „be freed from sudden death, which is the most terrible stroke launched by Divine Justice against sinners." *Qui Missam devote audierit subitanea morte non peribit.* (Sup. Can. *Quia passus, de Consecr.* dist. 2). „Behold a wonderful preservative," says the Saint, „against sudden death: attend holy Mass every day, and attend it with all possible devotion." He who carries with him so effective a guard, shall live secure against the occurrence of so terrific a misfortune. There has even existed a current popular opinion, attributed by some to St. Augustine, that, during the time of Mass, the human frame grows no older, but is maintained all the time in the same essential vigor in which it was at the commencement. I do not care to know whether this be true or not; but, at any rate, this I say, that if he who attends Mass grows older in respect of bodily age, the lapse of time during Mass leaves him at least no older in sin than he was: because, as St. Gregory says, „one who attends holy Mass with real devotion keeps in the direct way of the Spirit." *Justus audiens Missam in via rectitudinis conservatur* (*de Sac. Miss.* apud. Bern. de Bust.). Grace and merit are all the while increasing in him, and he makes ever new acquisitions of virtue, so as more and more to please his God. St. Bernard even sums it up thus, that more is to be gained in one single Mass (here we must understand him of its intrinsic value) than by distributing your means to the poor, or going on pilgrimages through all the most famous sanctuaries of the world. *Audiens devote Missam aut celebrans multo magis meretur, quam si substantiam suam pauperibus erogaret, et totam terram peregrinando transiret* (apud Bern. de Bust. p. 2, ser. 6). O unbounded riches of holy Mass! Grasp well this truth: it is possible for you to gain more favor with God by attending or celebrating one single Mass, considered in itself and in its intrinsic worth, than by opening the treasury of your wealth and distributing the whole to the poor, or by going as pilgrim over the whole world and visiting with utmost devotion the sanctuaries of Rome, of Compostella, of Loreto, Jerusalem, and the rest. And this most reasonably follows from the position laid down by the angelic St. Thomas, when he says that in Mass are contained all the fruits, all the graces, yea, all those immense treasures which the Son of God poured out so abundantly upon the Church, His Spouse, in the bloody sacrifice of the Cross. *In qualibet Missa invenitur omnis fructus et utilitas quam Christus in die Parasceves operatus est in cruce* (*de Consecr.* dist. 2).

Requiem æternam
dona eis Domine
et lux perpetua
luceat eis.
Requiescant in pace
Amen.

41

The Three Excellenceies of Mass
Part 3.

*N*ow, pause a little ----- close this book ----- read no further at pre-sent, but sum up in your mind all these singular uses of holy Mass, weigh them well in silence, and then tell me, will you have again a difficulty in believing that one single Mass ----- speaking of its own intrinsic worth and value ----- is of such efficacy as, according to the speculation of various learned men, might have sufficed to obtain the salvation of the whole human race? Imagine the case that Our Lord Jesus Christ had not suffered anything on Calvary and, in place of His bloody sacrifice of the Cross, had solely instituted Mass for our redemption, with an express command that in all the world it should only be celebrated once. Well, then, had this been the case, that single Mass, celebrated by the poorest priest in the world, would have been sufficient, considered in itself and so far as its own share in the work is concerned, to win from God the salvation of all men. Yes; one single Mass, taking the case imagined above, might thus have been made to obtain the conversion of all Mahometans, all heretics, all schismatics, in fine, of all unbelievers, and also that of all bad Christians; closing the gates of Hell to all sinners, and emptying Purgatory of all the souls there obtaining purification. We, unhappy creatures, through our tepidity, through our little devotion, and possibly even through our scandalous improprieties committed during attendance on Mass ----- oh, how we contract the limits of its vast circumference, and render ineffective its mighty worth! Would that I could climb the summits of the loftiest mountains, and thence exclaim aloud, „O nations deceived! O nations deceived! what are you about? Why run you not to the churches, there to listen with holy hearts to all the Masses in your power? Why not imitate the holy Angels, who, according to the saying of St. Chrysostom, when holy Mass is being celebrated, descend in squadrons from the empyrean, and stand before our altars, covered with the wings of reverential awe, waiting the whole of that blessed time, in order that they may intercede for us the more effectively, well knowing this to be the time most opportune, the conjuncture, above every other, propitious for obtaining favors from Heaven. Sink down, then, in confusion for having in time past so little appreciated holy Mass, for perhaps having even many times profaned an act so dread and holy; much more so if you are of the number of those who have recklessly dared to utter, „A Mass more or less is of little importance."

XVII.

And now, to end this instruction, reflect that I have not by mere chance dropped the expression that one Mass alone, so far as itself is concerned and in the sense of its own intrinsic value, is sufficient to empty Purgatory of all the Souls in process of purification, and place them in holy Paradise. For this Divine sacrifice not only avails for the Souls of the dead, as propitiatory and satisfactory of their penance (*De Lug.* s. 6, n. 158), but it also assists as a great act of supplication for them, conformably, you see, to the custom of the Church, which not only offers Mass for the Souls that are being purified, but prays during the sacrifice for their liberation. In order, then, that you may be stirred to compassion for the Holy Souls, know that the fire by which they are covered is one so devouring that, according to the opinion of St. Gregory, it is no less than that of Hell (Dial. 1. 4, c. 131), operating as the instrument of Divine justice with such force as to render their pains insufferable, greater than all the possible Martyrdoms that can be witnessed or felt, or even imagined, here below. Still more than all this, the pain of loss afflicts them because, deprived as they are of the Beatific Vision of God, they, as the Angelic Doctor says (in Dist. 12, art. 1), experience an intolerable passion, an intense and vivid desire to behold the Supreme Good, and this is not permitted to them. Enter here into yourself and ponder. If you should see your father or your mother on the point of being drowned, and if to save them would not cost you more than the stretching out of your hand, would not you feel bound by every law of charity and of justice to extend that hand to aid them? How then? You behold with the eyes of faith so many Poor Souls, and perhaps your nearest and dearest, in a lake of flame, and you will not endure a little inconvenience in order to attend devoutly, for their help, one single Mass! What sort of heart is yours? I do not doubt that holy Mass not only shortens their pains, but also extends great immediate relief to these Poor Souls. It has even been thought by some that while Mass is being celebrated for a soul, the fire, otherwise most devouring, suspends its rigor, and no pain is suffered by that Soul during all the time that the holy sacrifice proceeds. We may well believe, at least, that at every Mass many issue forth from Purgatory and fly to holy Paradise. Add this consideration, that the charity which you exercise toward Poor Souls under purification will all redound to your own good. Examples without end might be adduced in confirmation of this truth, but one most authentic will suffice. St. Peter Damian, when left an orphan by his parents, and yet of tender age, was placed in the house of one of his brothers, who gave him the worst of usage, to the extent of making him go barefoot and in rags; in short, causing him to endure in every way the extremest penury. He happened one day to find on the road a piece of money, I know not what. Think whether he rejoiced or not! He seemed to himself to have found a treasure; but how to spend it? His necessities suggested many ways. At last, after thinking and rethinking, he resolved to give it to a priest, that he might celebrate a Mass for the Holy Souls in Purgatory. From that time forward, the scenes of his fortune changed. He was taken home by another brother of better dispositions, who loved him as his son, clothed him with propriety, and sent him to school, whence he finally came forth that great man, and great Saint, who was the ornament of the purple and so effective a prop of the Church. Now you see how from one single Mass, obtained at a slight personal inconvenience, all this happiness originated. O blessed Mass! at once assisting the living and the dead, beneficial for time and for eternity! For you must know that the Holy Souls are so grateful to their benefactors that, when once in Heaven, they constitute themselves their advocates, nor will they ever rest till they see them also in possession of glory. It would seem that an unworthy woman in Rome experienced this. Utterly forgetful of her eternal salvation, she had no other heed than to give vent to evil passions, and to ruin youth; nor did she do any good, except that every few days she would get a Mass for Souls in Purgatory. It was they, as we may well believe, who so interceded for their benefactress that one day she was overtaken by vehement contrition for her sins. Abandoning her infamous dwelling, she sped to the feet of a zealous confessor, made her general confession, and soon after died in such good dispositions that she afforded to one and all clear signs of eternal salvation. This grace so altogether miraculous was generally attributed to the virtue of those Masses celebrated at her request, in behalf of the blessed Souls in Purgatory. Let us then awake, and heed lest we permit that *publicani et meretrices praecedent nos in regnum Dei* ----- „lest publicans and the harlots shall go into the kingdom of God before us" (St. Matt. xxi. 31).

XVIII.

If I thought there was a chance of your being one of those so sunk in avarice, as not only to fail in charity by neglecting prayer for their friends departed, never hearing a single Mass for their poor suffering Souls, but even trampling on every dictate of justice, by refusing to fulfill the pious legacies of their predecessors, or who, being priests, accumulate obligations to offer Masses, without ever doing so; oh, that I could take fire to cast at you, saying to your face ----- Away with you, worse than devil! after all, devils only torment reprobate souls, but you torment the spirits of the elect; devils are only cruel to those foreknown by God as lost, but you to the predestined, the loved of God. No; for you there is neither confession that avails, nor absolution that is valid, nor confessor that can absolve, unless you do great penance for so great a sin, and accurately satisfy all your obligations toward the departed. „But, my father, I cannot; I have not the means." Cannot? have not the means? For all this external show there seems to be means; for extravagance of luxury you have means; for so much parade there are means; for the cost of parties, and of feasts, for filling country-houses with company, for haunts of dissipation and even of vice, it would seem that you both have and can. And to satisfy positive debts not only to the living, but what is more, to the poor departed, how dare you say you have not, and cannot? Well, then, I understand you: but hearken, though there is none on earth who sees these accounts, you have yet to settle them with God. Give yourself up, if you will, to devouring the legacies of the dead, the pious destinations for Masses and for charities, but know that for you there stands registered in the oracle of the prophet a threatening of woe, malediction, misfortune, and ruin irreparable, in property, life, and reputation. It is the voice of God, and cannot fail: *Comederunt sacrificia mortuorum, et multipli-*

cata est in eis ruina (Ps. cv. 28, 29). Yes, ruin, misfortune, downfall irrecoverable to that house which does not satisfy its obligations to the dead! Take a turn through Rome, and behold the many families scattered, houses gone to decay, warehouses closed, enterprises suspended, trades at a stand ----- what failures, calamities, and miseries! O poor ruined Rome! you say. But what is the cause of so much decay? If you scrutinize exactly these disasters, you will find, among many sins, one chief cause to be this very cruelty to the departed, this refusal of the help due to them, this negligence in satisfying pious destinations of property; and, further, because thus there have come to be committed infinite sacrileges; the holy sacrifice profaned, and the temple of God, as the Redeemer said, turned into a den of thieves. What wonder, if Heaven rain lightnings, and seem to threaten wars, earthquakes, and extermination ----- for behold, *Comederunt sacrificia mortuorum, et multiplicata est in eis ruina.* Most justly were such ungrateful men declared by the fourth Council of Carthage to be excommunicate, as true murderers of their kin, and by the Valensian Council to be practically infidels, that must be driven out from the Church. But this is far from the greatest chastisement inflicted by Almighty God on hearts grown cold to departed friends. Ah, the flood of woe reserved for them in the other life! According to the declaration of St. James, such souls shall be judged by God without pity, since they exercised none: *judicium sine misericordia illi qui non fecit misericordiam* (St. James, ii. 13). God will permit them in their turn to be paid in their own coin; no last wishes of theirs shall be fulfilled, no Masses celebrated for their souls, though provided for in their testaments; or if celebrated, they will not be accepted by God, but will be applied by Him to other Souls in need, who in life had compassion on the poor departed. Thus we read in the chronicles of our Order, of a friar who, after death, appeared to one of his companions, and manifested to him the bitter pain he was enduring in Purgatory, particularly for having been very negligent toward the other departed brothers, and how, up to that time, all that had been done in his behalf, the Masses themselves that had been celebrated, had all availed him nothing; because Almighty God, in punishment of his neglect, had applied them to other Souls, who, in life, had acted well by those under purification; this said, he disappeared (*Cron. Fratr. Min.* part 2).

XIX.

Before concluding the present instruction, permit me, with knees bent to the earth and with joined hands, to supplicate you who read, not to shut this little book without first making a solid resolution of applying for the future your most strenuous diligence to attend and also to get celebrated all the Masses possible in your circumstances, not only for the Souls of the departed, but also for your own. SAINT MECHTIL-DEDo this from two motives: first, to obtain a good and holy death ----- it being the invariable opinion of theologians that there is no more efficacious means than Mass for attaining so holy a purpose. Christ Our Lord is said to have revealed to St. Mechtilde (1. 3, Grat. Spiro c. 27) that he who in life is in the habit of devoutly hearing holy Mass shall in death be consoled by the presence of the Angels and Saints, his advocates, who shall bravely defend him from all the snares of infernal spirits. Oh, how beautiful the death which is destined to succeed your life, if you shall have striven to hear with devotion as many Masses as you could! Another motive is that you may yourself issue quickly from Purgatory and flyaway into eternal glory, there being no means more adapted for obtaining from God a grace so precious as that of going direct to Heaven, or at least of short detention on the way, than Indulgences duly gained, and the holy sacrifice. As for Indulgences, the Supreme Pontiffs have opened their hands, and liberally concede many to those who hear holy Mass devoutly; and as to the efficacy of the most Holy Sacrifice of the Mass for accelerating the remission of the pains of Purgatory, it is already sufficiently shown. The example and authority of that great servant of God, [St.] John of Avila, the oracle of Spain, should suffice. Being asked on his death-bed what he had most at heart, and what kindness he most longed for after death, he answered, „Masses, Masses." I should wish in this matter to offer you, with your permission, an advice of great importance.

It is this: to procure that all the Masses which you would like to have celebrated for you after death shall be of fact celebrated for you during life, nor to trust to those who remain after you on the scene of this world. You will think the more of this counsel, from St. Anselm declaring that one single Mass heard or celebrated for your soul during life may perhaps be more profitable to you than a thousand after death: *Audire devote unicam Missam „ in vita, vel dare eleemosynam pro ea, prodest magis quam relinquere ad celebrandum mille post obitum.*" (Apud Castell, diur. sac. Praep.) Well was this truth understood by a rich merchant of the cost of Genoa, who at his death left nothing in suffrage for his soul. Every one was astonished how a man so rich, so pious, and so generous toward all, could have proved at death so cruel to himself. But after his burial there was found a record in one of his little books of the good which he had done for his soul during life: „Masses caused to be celebrated for my soul, two thousand lire;" „for the marriage of poor girls, ten thousand;" „two hundred for such and such a holy place;" and so on. And at the end of this little book was written: „He who desires good, let him do good in life, and not trust to the fidelity of those left behind at death." ----- -" A taper before lights better than a torch behind." Make use of the noble example just recorded, and, having thoroughly pondered the excellence of holy Mass, wonder at the blindness in which you have lived till now, having formed no right estimate of a treasure which has for you too much remained, as it were, hidden and buried. Now, therefore, that you know its value, banish from your mind, and still more from your tongue, the monstrous thought that „a Mass more or less matters little;" or „that it is no small thing to hear Mass on festivals;" or „that the Mass of this or that priest is like a Mass of Holy Week for length; when he appears at the altar it is high time to get out of church." Renew also your holy resolution to hear from this time forward as many Masses as you possibly can, and, above all, with due devotion. To succeed, make use of the practical and devout method which follows; and may God bless you.

St. Francis of Assisi Adoring the Christ Child
by Denys Calvaert, 1607

Chapter 2

Devout Method of Hearing Mass

I.

*I*t was the opinion of Chrysostom (Homil. 3, incomp. Dei. Nat.), in harmony with that which has just been taught in the preceding instruction, and his opinion was confirmed by St. Gregory in the fourth of his Dialogues, that while holy Mass is being celebrated by the priest, the heavens open and there descend from the empyrean many bands of Angels to assist at the Divine sacrifice. St. Nilus the Abbot, disciple of the aforesaid St. John Chrysostom, avers of that holy Doctor of the Church that, while celebrating, he saw about the altar a great multitude of those heavenly spirits, assisting the sacred ministers in their holy function. Behold, then, the most proper method of assisting with fruit at holy Mass. Go to the church as if you were going to Calvary, and behave yourself before the altar as before the throne of God, in company with the holy Angels. See what modesty, what reverence, what attention, are requisite from us in order that we may carry away the fruit and the blessings which Almighty God is wont to bestow on him who honors with devout demeanor these sacred mysteries.

II.

We read that while the sacrifices of the Old Law were being offered by the Jews, sacrifices in which was offered nothing greater than bulls, lambs, and other animals, it was admirable to behold with what diligence, decorum, and silence the whole people assisted; and although there were numbers innumerable of those attending, besides the seven hundred ministers who sacrificed, yet, with all this, it seemed as if the temple were empty, not the very slightest noise, not even a breath, being heard. Now, if so much respect and so much veneration were practised toward those sacrifices which, after all, were only a mere shadow, a simple figure of ours, what silence, what devotion, what attention, does not holy Mass deserve, in which the Immaculate Lamb Himself, the Divine Word, is offered for us in sacrifice! Well did the glorious St. Ambrose understand this, who, as Cesarius narrates (1. 2. Mirac. c. 40), while celebrating holy Mass, used, after reading the Gospel, to turn round to the people, exhort all to devout recollection, and enjoin a most rigorous silence, not only to the extent of abstaining from the slightest syllable, but also from coughing, moving, and every sort of sound. He was obeyed, and whoever assisted at his Mass used to feel ravished by a holy dread, and was interiorly moved so as to carry away great fruit and much increase of grace.

III.

Such, too, is the object of this little work, which has no higher pretension than to move those who shall be pleased to read it to embrace with fervor of spirit the practice and method of hearing holy Mass, which has now been described. And since the methods of assisting at holy Mass which have hitherto been taught are so various, and all so devout and holy, as we see in the many little books sent to press with this view, to the great profit of the faithful, I mean to do no violence to your choice, but leave you to choose that which shall seem most agreeable to your devout dispositions, and to your capacity. I shall only attempt the office of the angel guardian, and merely suggest to you the method which, according to my feeble judgment, may turn out the most useful and the least difficult. For this purpose I shall divide the common subject into three classes.

IV.

The first method of hearing holy Mass is used by those who, book in hand, accompany with the utmost attention all the actions of the priest, repeat at each of these a vocal prayer, as laid down in the book, and thus pass the whole of Mass reading; and there is no doubt that if this be united with a right consideration of the sacred mysteries, it is a most excellent method of assisting at the holy sacrifice, and of great spiritual fruit. But as it involves an entire bondage, requiring the worshipper to attend to V.

V.

The second method of hearing holy Mass is that employed by those who dispense with books, who read nothing whatsoever during the time of the divine sacrifice, but fixing their mental eye, kindled by faith, on Jesus crucified, and leaning against the tree of the cross, gather its fruits in sweet contemplation, pass the whole time in devout interior recollection, and sweetly engage their minds in consideration of those sacred mysteries of the Passion of Jesus, which is not only represented, but is mystically carried out, in that holy sacrifice. It is certain that such, keeping their faculties gathered up in God, arrive at the exercise of heroic acts of faith, hope, charity, and other virtues; and there is no doubt that this mode of hearing Mass is much more profitable than the first, as well as more sweet and attractive. This was experienced by a good lay brother (Hom. in. Inquis.), who used to say that in hearing Mass he only read three letters. The first was black; that is to say, the consideration of his sins, which caused in him confusion and repentance, and thus he meditated from the beginning of Mass to the Offertory. The second was red; that is, the meditation on the Passion of Jesus, contemplating that most precious blood which Jesus shed for us on Calvary, when He suffered a death so bitter: and in this he engaged his mind till the Communion. The third was white; because, while the priest communicated, he united himself mentally with his Jesus in the sacrament, making a spiritual Communion, after which he remained all absorbed in God, thinking of the glory for which he hoped, as fruit of the divine sacrifice. This plain, simple soul heard Mass with much perfection; and I wish that all might learn from him a wisdom so sublime.

VI.

The third method of hearing holy Mass with profit consists of a course between the two just now described, neither requiring you to read many vocal prayers, as is prescribed in the first, nor calling for a very elevated spirit of contemplation, such as is aimed at by those who follow the second. But if you consider it well, you will find it to be the one best conformed to the spirit of the Church, which enjoins that we unite our thoughts with those of the celebrant, who ought to offer the sacrifice for those four ends indicated in the preceding instruction, this being, according to the declaration of the Angelic Doctor, the most efficacious method of paying the four great debts owing by us to God. Now, since you yourself exercise in a certain manner the office of priest when you assist at Mass, you should be actuated as much as possible by consideration of these four ends; and this will be easy if you but practice during the time of Mass the four offerings, as they shall shortly be described. Here is the practical form clearly prepared for you. Carry for some time with you this little book, till you have quite learned the forms of offering, or at least have become thoroughly well imbued with their sense, since it is not important that you should cling particularly to the words; and so soon as Mass commences, while the priest humbles himself at the foot of the altar, saying the *Confiteor*, etc., do you then, after a brief self-examination, stir up your heart to true contrition, asking pardon of God for your sins, and beseeching the aid of the Holy Spirit, and the intercession of most blessed Mary, that you may hear this Mass with all reverence and devotion. Then divide it into four spaces of time, in order to pay during these, as follows, the four great obligations before mentioned.

VII.

In the first part, which shall be from the beginning to the Gospel, you will strive to acquit yourself to the obligation of honoring and praising the majesty of that God Who is worthy of infinite honor and praise. Wherefore, humble yourself with Jesus, and plunge yourself down in thought into the depth of your nothingness; confess sincerely how wretched and how merely nothing you are before so immense a majesty; and thus humbled internally and externally, and remaining, as you ought throughout Mass, all modest and composed, repeat the following words:

„O my God, I adore Thee, and acknowledge Thee for my Lord, and for master of my soul. I protest that all I am, and all I have, are willingly acknowledged by me to be from Thee. And since Thy Supreme Majesty deserves infinite honor and homage, while I am but a poor, helpless being, utterly incapable of paying so great a debt, I offer up to Thee the humiliation and the homage which Jesus renders to Thee on the altar. That which Jesus does I purpose also to do. I humble, I abase myself, together with Him, before Thy Majesty. I adore Thee with the same humiliation which Jesus practises, and I rejoice and am glad that blessed Jesus should give to Thee, in my behalf, infinite honor and homage."

Then close the book, and pursue the exercise of forming many such internal acts of joy, that God should thus be infinitely honored. Repeat, over and over again: „Yes, my God, I delight in the infinite honor which results to Thy Majesty from this holy sacrifice. I delight in it; I rejoice as much as I know how, as much as I can." Nor be at all anxious to keep to the words just given, but make use of those which your devotion shall dictate while you remain all gathered up in, and united with, God. This will indeed be a happy fulfillment of the first of your obligations.

VIII.

In the second interval, that is, from the Gospel to the Elevation, you will acquit yourself of the second obligation. Casting a brief glance and recognizing the immeasurable nature of your debt toward Divine Justice, say with humbled heart:

„Behold, my God, this traitor who hath so many times rebelled against Thee. Ah, me! pierced with grief, how I abominate and detest my heavy sins, while I offer for them that same satisfaction which Jesus offers on the altar. I offer to Thee all the merits of Jesus, all Jesus Himself, God and man, Who now, as an unbloody Victim, pleads anew for me His bloody sacrifice on the Cross. I offer all that He does on that altar as my Mediator and Advocate, imploring of Thee to pardon me through His most Precious Blood. I unite myself with the cry of that loving Blood, and I beseech of Thee mercy for my sins, so grievous and so many. The blood of Jesus cries for mercy; my pierced heart cries for mercy! Ah! dear God, if my tears move Thee not, let the groans of my Jesus move Thee; that mercy which He obtained for the whole human race on the Cross, why should He not obtain it for me on this altar? Yes, yes; I hope that, in virtue of that most Precious Blood, Thou wilt pardon all my most grievous transgressions, for which I shall persevere in weeping to the last breath of my life."

Shutting the book, repeat many of these acts of true, intimate, and vehement contrition. Then give rein to your affections, and without sound of words, but within your heart, say to Jesus: „O dearest Jesus, give me the tears of Peter, the contrition of Magdalene, and the grief of those Saints who, once sinners, were afterward true penitents, in order that in this Mass I may obtain a general pardon of my sins." Make many such acts, entirely gathered up in God, and be sure that in this way you will fully discharge the debt of your many sins.

IX.

During the third space of time ----- from the Elevation till Communion, stir your soul to wonder at the overflowing torrent of great and good gifts either bestowed on you or designed for you by God, and then offer to Him in return a gift of infinite value, that is, the Body and Blood of „See me, my most beloved God, laden with the benefits, both general and particular, which Thou deignest to bestow on me in time, and to store up for me in eternity. I know that Thy mercies toward me have been and are infinite, but yet I am ready to repay Thee all, even to the last farthing. Behold, I thank and repay Thee by this most Precious Body, this Divine Blood, this innocent Victim, which I present to Thee by the hands of Thy priest. I am certain that this offering which I make is sufficient to repay all the gifts Thou hast bestowed on me. This gift of infinite value is by itself worth all the gifts which I have received, which I do now receive, and am yet to receive from Thee. Ah, holy Angels, and all you beloved ones in Heaven, help me to thank my God, and to offer Him, in thanksgiving for such benefits, not only this but all the Masses which are being actually celebrated throughout the whole world, in order that His loving beneficiaries may remain fulyly recompensed for so many graces which he hath bestowed on me, which He is now about to bestow, and will bestow throughout eternal ages. Amen."

Oh, how will our good God be pleased with thanks so affectionate! Oh, how satisfied will He remain with this sole offering ----- worth all other offerings, since it is of infinite worth! And to stir yourself the more to feelings so devout, invite all heaven in like manner to employ itself for you; invoke all those saints to whom you feel the greatest devotion, and say to them, with the inner voice of your heart, „O dear ones, my very holy advocates, thank for me the goodness of my God, so that I may not live and die without utterance of my gratitude. Ah, beseech Him to accept the impulse of my heart, and to have regard to the loving thanks offered by my Jesus for me in this Mass." Nor content yourself with speaking thus once only, but repeat it over and over again, and be assured that in this way, you will make great approaches toward satisfying this obligation. Still more will you succeed if every morning you make the Act of Offering which commences „Eternal God," etc., (HERE) offering with this view all the Masses that are being celebrated at the time throughout the world.

X.

In the fourth space of time ----- from the Communion to the end ----- after having made a spiritual Communion while the priest communicated sacramentally, in the manner which I shall suggest at the end of this chapter, look upon God Who is within you, and then summon up holy courage to ask of Him many graces, knowing that at that time Jesus unites Himself to you, and prays and supplicates ----- yes, even He ----- in your behalf; and therefore enlarge your heart, and do not ask things of small importance, but ask great graces, your offering being so great, namely, that of His Divine Son. Say to Him with a humble heart: „O my dearest God, too well I recognize myself as unworthy of Thy favors. I confess my supreme unworthiness, and that because of so many and so grievous sins I deserve not to be heard. But how shalt Thou be able to refuse attention to Thy Divine Son Who on yon altar prays for me, and offers to Thee, in my behalf, His life and His Blood? Ah, my God, my most beloved, hear the prayer of this my great Advocate, and for His sake grant me all the graces which Thou knowest to be necessary for accomplishing the great affair of my eternal salvation. And now that I take heart to ask of Thee a general pardon of all my sins, and the grace of final perseverance, I also ask of Thee, my God, trusting in the merits and intercession of my Jesus, all virtues in a heroic degree, and all the aids efficacious for making me a true Saint. I ask of Thee the conversion of all unbelievers and of all sinners, and particularly of those who belong to me by the ties of blood or by spiritual affinity. I beg of Thee the liberation, not of one soul only, but of all the souls in purgatory. Oh, bring them all out, so that, through the efficacy of this divine sacrifice, that prison where they are being rendered pure may become empty. Convert also all the souls of the living; may this miserable world become a paradise of delight for Thee, where, loved, reverenced, and praised in time by all of us, we may come afterward to praise and bless Thee for all eternity. Amen."

Offer petitions also again and again for yourself, your children, your friends, relations, and acquaintance; ask help for all your needs, both spiritual and temporal; ask also the fulness of all good, and relief from all evils for holy Church: and do not ask any of these things with lukewarmness, but rather with a great confidence, making sure that your prayers, united with those of Jesus, shall indeed be heard. Then, holy Mass being ended, make an act of thanksgiving to God in the words, *Agimus tibi gratias*, etc.; and leave church with a contrite heart, as if you were coming down from Calvary.

Now tell me, if all the Masses which you have heard till now had been heard by you in this manner, with how many treasures would not you have enriched your soul? Oh, the loss you have suffered while you have been present at holy Mass, but looking here and there, observing who came in or went out; sometimes even talking, or being half asleep, or, at most, mumbling wretchedly a few vocal prayers without one whit of interior recollection. Resolve, then, to embrace this most sweet and easy way of hearing Mass with profit, which consists in paying the four great debts due to God, and be very sure that in a short time you will make an abundant acquisition of the rarest graces. After trying this plan, it will never again enter your mind to say, „A Mass more or less is of no consequence."

XI.

As for the way of making a spiritual Communion at the time when the priest communicates at Mass, as was alluded to above, it behooves one to know the doctrine laid down by the holy Council of Trent, which says that men may receive the Holy Sacrament in three manners: the first, only sacramentally; the second, only spiritually; the third, both sacramentally and spiritually. Here I shall not speak of the first, which is the Communion of those who communicate in a state of mortal sin, as Judas did, nor of the third, which is the case of those who really communicate, and do so in a state of grace; but I speak of the second, which, as the sacred Council says, is peculiar to those ----- *Qui voto propositum ilium caelestem Panem edentes, fide viva, quae per dilectionem operatur, fructum ejus, et utilitatem sentiunt* (Sess. xiii. c. 8) ----- „who not being able to receive sacramentally the body of the Lord, receive Him spiritually, with acts of living faith and fervent charity, and with a supreme desire of uniting themselves to that supreme good, thus rendering themselves capable of receiving the fruit of this Divine Sacrament."

In order to facilitate a practice of such great excellence, ponder what I have to say. When the priest is about to give himself Communion in holy Mass, do you, keeping composed externally and internally, excite in your heart an act of true contrition, and humbly striking your breast, in token that you acknowledge yourself unworthy of so great a grace, make all those acts of love, of self-surrender, of humility, and the rest, which you are accustomed to make when you communicate sacramentally, and then desire with a lively longing to receive your good Jesus, veiled in the Sacrament for your benefit. And to kindle your devotion, imagine that most holy Mary, or some Saint, your holy advocate, is holding forth to you the sacred particle; figure yourself receiving it, and then, embracing Jesus in your heart, reply to Him, over and over again, with interior words prompted by love: „Come, Jesus, my beloved, come within this my poor heart; come and satiate my desires; come and sanctify my soul; come, most sweet Jesus, come!" This said, be still; contemplate your good God within you, and, as if you really had communicated, adore Him, thank Him, and perform all those interior acts to which you are accustomed after sacramental

Communion.

Now, learn that this blessed and holy spiritual Communion, so little practised by the Christians of our day, is a treasure capable of filling the soul with a thousand benefits; and, as various authors say (Rodriguez, Exerc. Perf. p. 2, tract. 8, c. 15), „is so useful that it is capable of producing the same graces which sacramental Communion produces; nay, in some cases more. For although, indeed, sacramental Communion, that is, when the sacred particle is really received, is of its own nature equal to the production of a higher result; because, being the Sacrament, it possesses virtue ex opere operato, nevertheless, a soul may make a spiritual Communion with so much humility, love, and devotion, as to win greater grace than another soul communicating sacramentally but without dispositions so thoroughly perfect.

Our Saviour testifies so much favor to this spiritual Communion that on many occasions He has been pleased to respond with evident miracles to the pious longings of His servants; now communicating them with His Own hands, as occurred to the Blessed Clare of Montefalco, St. Catharine of Siena, and St. Lydwina; now by the hands of Angels, as to my patron St. Bonaventure, called the Seraphic Doctor, and to two holy bishops, Onoratus and Firminus; sometimes by means of the great and blessed Mother of God, who desired to communicate the Blessed Silvester with her own hands. Nor should you marvel at these ingenuities of love; because spiritual Communion inflames the soul with the love of God, unites it with Him, and disposes it to receive the most signal favors. Reflecting, then, on this truth, how can you ever remain so cold and insensible? And what excuse can you ever adduce for exempting yourself from a practice so devout? Ah, decide once for all to adopt it henceforward, considering farther that such holy spiritual Commuion gives you at least this one advantage over sacramental Communion, that the latter is only possible once each day, while the former may be as frequent as the Masses you attend; nay, may be repeated at other times, morning, noon, and eve, in church or at home, and this without need of permission from your confessor. In short, so often as you practise what has been now prescribed, so often may you make a spiritual Communion, and thus become enriched with graces and merits of every kind and degree of excellence.

Now, then, you have had laid before you the whole object of this slight little treatise. It is simply to plant in the hearts of all those who shall read it a holy desire that there may be introduced into the Catholic world the practice of hearing holy Mass every day with the most solid piety and devotion, and that each time Mass is heard each hearer may make a spiritual Communion. Oh, the gain if this end were attained! I should then hope to witness, throughout the whole world, that holy fervor flourishing once more which was admired in the golden age of the primitive Church, when the faithful assisted every day at the holy sacrifice, and every day communicated sacramentally. If you are not worthy of such a privilege, oh, at least hear holy Mass every day, and every day communicate spiritually. If I succeed in gaining you who read me now, I shall imagine myself to have gained the whole world, and I shall consider my poor labor well laid out.

But in order to take away all the excuses which are wont to be brought forward by some for not hearing holy Mass, there shall be adduced, in the following chapter, various examples adapted to every sort of person, to show that, if they deprive themselves of so great a good, it is by their own fault, their tepidity, their weariness in well-doing; and that great indeed shall be their remorse on this account at the point of death.

Chapter 3

On Hearing Mass Daily
Part 1.: For Priests Except in Case of
Just Impediment

*M*any are the excuses which those who attend holy Mass grudgingly and with reluctance find for their tepidity. You may observe them all immersed in business, all anxious and intent (to use a common and most accurate expression) on promoting „their own dirty interests." For these, every fatigue is a trifle; nor is there any inconvenience which they will allow to stand in their way; while, for attending holy Mass, which is the great affair of all, you will perceive them languid, cold, with a hundred frivolous pretexts at hand about important occupations, weak health, family troubles, want of time, multiplicity of business, and so on. In short, if holy Church did not oblige them under pain of mortal sin to frequent the Divine mysteries at least on festivals, God knows if ever they would visit a church, or bend a knee before the altar. Oh, shame and utter disgrace to our times! Miserable that we are! How have we declined from the fervor of those first believers who, as I said before, every day assisted at the adorable sacrifice, and refreshed their souls with the Bread of Angels, communicating sacramentally! And yet they also were not without transactions and business and occupations; nay, by this very means their temporal business and interests, as well as their spiritual, got on all the better. Blind world, when wilt thou open thine eyes to recognize delusions so gross? Up, and awaken, one and all! Be this your most sweet and beloved devotion ----- to hear holy Mass every morning, and to accompany it by a spiritual Communion. To gain this end with you, I know no method more efficacious than example, it being an irrefragable maxim, *Vivimus ab exemplo*; and everything is rendered easy and pleasant which we see done by our companions or equals. Tu non poteris, said St. Augustine, accusing himself, *tu non poteris quod* *isti et istae?* (Confes. 1, 8, c. 11.) We shall, therefore, adduce several examples, bearing reference to various classes of persons, hoping thus at last to win all.

An instance which came under my own observation will explain the first part of what I have to say to priests. A priest, by reason of a violent blow on the fingers of his right hand, was prevented celebrating for two months. From saving Mass as formerly every day, never once omitting it, he now did not even communicate, though there occurred several high festivals; nor did he even attend Mass on days which were not of obligation. And why? I blush to hint that for merely going to holy Communion, or simply attending Mass, there was no motive of gain which could come into play. How can one express the horror due to such a state of soul? Truly some offering is due to the priest who celebrates, because, qui altari inservit de altari vivere debet ----- „he who serves the altar shall live by the altar;" but it is necessary to say that this can never be the main object of a good priest ----- such offerings can never be justly given or received in the spirit of purchase. Stir yourselves up, then, O priests of Christ, and make it your first point to be pure and single of eye, your intentions being entirely referred to God. For this end, before commencing holy Mass, renew, at least mentally, the four ends indicated above, and prescribed by the Angelic Doctor. Then in your mementos, after applying the sacrifice for those to whom you are under that obligation, make briefly the offerings aforesaid to the Most High, directing your act to those holy ends for which it was primarily spirit, and making throughout internal efforts corresponding to their holy suggestions. Then truly will there be an influx of great devotion into those assisting, and he will obtain the utmost profit for his own soul.

Now, on the supposition that such will be his method of celebrating, let every priest adopt the steadfast resolution of offering the adorable sacrifice every morning of his life; for if in the primitive Church the laity communicated daily, with how much more reason must we believe that the priesthood celebrated daily? *Quotidie immolo Deo Agnum Immaculatum*, said St. Andrew the Apostle to the tyrant; „daily I offer the Immaculate Lamb to God" (ex Sur. 38, Nov.). And St. Cyprian, in one of his epistles, says, *Sacerdotes qui Sacrificium Deo quotidie im-*

molamus ----- „we priests who celebrate and daily offer the sacrifice to God" (Ep. 54). And St. Gregory the Great (Hom. 27, in Evang.) narrates of St. Cassius, Bishop of Narni, that, being wont to say Mass daily, Almighty God commanded one of his chaplains to say to him, as from Heaven, that he did well, that his devotion was very pleasing, and that He laid up a reward for him above. But, on the other hand, as to those priests who through mere negligence fail to celebrate, who shall ever be able to calculate the loss which they inflict upon the whole Church? The maxim of the Venerable Bede is well known: *Sacerdos qui absque legitimo, impedimento missae celebration em omittit, quantum in ipso est, Sanctissimam Trinitatem privat laude et gloria, angelos laetitia, peccatores venia, justos auxilio et gratia, existentes in purgatorio subsidio et refrigerio, Ecclesiam ipsam ingenti beneficio, et seipsum medicina et remedio* ----- „the priest who, without legitimate impediment, fails to celebrate daily, deprives, so far as he can, the Most Holy Trinity of praise and glory, the Angels of joy, sinners of pardon, the good of help and grace, the Souls in Purgatory of succor and refreshment, the Church herself of immense benefit, and his own soul of medicine and remedy." Where will you find me a robber so notorious as at one stroke to execute a theft on such a scale as the priest who thus robs of blessing the living, the dead, and the whole Church? Nor can the excuse of occupation avail. The Blessed Ferdinand, Archbishop of Grenada, who was at the same time prime minister, and consequently immersed in public affairs, yet celebrated every morning. The Cardinal of Toledo gave him a hint (Rodriguez, Exerc. Perf. p. 2, tract. 7, c. 16) that the court murmured against him for celebrating daily, oppressed as he was with business. „For that matter," replied the servant of God, „your highness having imposed a burden so exorbitant on my shoulders, I can find no better support against sinking to the ground than the holy sacrifice of Mass, from which I extract strength for the office laid upon me." Much less avails a certain sort of humility. St. Peter Celestine, from the great conception he had of the loftiness of such a function, was once disposed to cease celebrating daily, when there appeared to him a holy abbot (Sur. in Vito ipsius. c. 3), from whom he had received the habit of a monk, and who thus addressed him in an authoritative manner: „What seraph in all Heaven will you find worthy to celebrate Mass? Almighty God has made, not Angels, but men, the ministers of the holy sacrifice, and as men they are subject to a thousand imperfections. Humble yourself; yes, but celebrate daily, for such is the will of God." And since repetition does not of itself diminish reverence, you should force yourself to copy those Saints who most excelled in modesty and attention during a function so holy. The great and celebrated Archbishop Saint Herbert was ever, while celebrating, touched with a devotion so extraordinary that he seemed an Angel of Paradise. The Blessed St. Lawrence Justinian, in offering holy Mass, became fixed and rigid, his eyes bedewed with tears, his spirit all rapt in God. But above all may St. Francis of Sales be cited as an example. Never was there an ecclesiastic seen who stood before the altar with greater majesty, with greater awe, reverence, and recollection, than that which shone conspicuous in him. Scarcely was he habited in the sacerdotal vestments, than he cast aside every other thought; and, once his foot was placed on the first step of the altar, his whole being, interior and exterior, assumed an angelic state, which carried away with devotion whoever beheld him.

But how came it that these Saints found so great a spiritual nourishment in celebrating the Divine mysteries? Because they did so as if they saw with their very eyes that they were in the presence of the whole court of heaven, as I believe to have once literally happened to St. Bonitus, Bishop of Claremont. It is told that, being one night alone in church, he beheld the Blessed Virgin, and a great company of Saints, some of whom asked their heavenly Lady, „Who is to celebrate at dawn?" She replied, „Bonitus, my dear servant;" and he became aware that morning at Mass that he was celebrating in presence of the great Mother of God, and of all those citizens of heaven. After Mass, the most holy Virgin gave him a snow-white alb, of texture so fine that there is nothing to compare to it, and preserved to our day as a precious relic. Think of the decorum, the recollection, and the love with which he must have celebrated that Mass! But if this example seem to you too sublime, contemplate as a model the glorious St. Vincent Ferrer, who celebrated daily before preaching, and made a point to aim at two perfections with which to approach the altar, namely, a consummate interior purity on his own part, and an extreme exterior cleanliness and propriety in everything connected with the sacred ceremonies. To obtain the first he confessed every morning; and this I would have of you, O priests, who seek in high degrees to taste of God while conducting the majestic mysteries. Some spend their half-hour or so in reading little manuals of devotion, in preparation for the adorable sacrifice, forgetful that with a brief self-examination, and by stirring up within them a true grief for some sin or other of their former life (if unable to discover other sufficient matter), they might in confession acquire great purity of heart. Behold the most noble preparation you can possibly make for holy Mass: every morning make your confession. Away with all scruples, and do not condemn my counsel! Oh, how much you will thank me when we shall find ourselves together in the home of a blessed eternity!

The aforesaid illustrious Saint always had the altar adorned with all the splendor in his power; and celebrating, as he usually did, before an immense crowd, he required the most perfect cleanliness and propriety in all the vestments, altar linens, and various furnishings of the sanctuary. For my poor part, I could shed tears when, during my missions, I find in so many churches, not only of villages, but of great cities also, vestments, corporals, purificatories, and other altar linens, so squalid, so stained and filthy, through the sordid avarice or the negligence and irreligion of the clergy, as to cause disgust to the mere senses, and to fill with horror, not only priests, but laity. *Nimis videtur absurdum*, says the holy Council of Lateran, *in sacris sordes negligere, quae dedecerent etiam in profanis.* (C. relinqui de custod. Euch.) I cannot endure such gross disorders. Sacristans, rectors, and parish priests, I hereby summon you before the tribunal of God, to render an account of indecencies so horrible. Who can exculpate you from serious breach of duty, if you supply the altar of God with what you would contemptuously reject in the case of an earthly table? And you, what are you about, bishops, dignitaries, and visitors? Why, when in your visitations you find unclean purificatories, corporals among which, perhaps, mice may have got, and veils unseamed, why do you not strike the faces of such parish clergy? Why do you not punish them with the utmost rigor? Perhaps you will say that during your visitations you find all right and proper. You let yourselves be deceived. Try the stratagem of a most zealous prelate, who found himself, during a visitation, in a sacristy provided handsomely with all things, gold brocades, fine albs, fine surplices, and altar-cloths of proportionate value.

„Now," said he to the parish priest, „I hereby forbid you, under pain of suspension, *a divinis ipso facto incurrenda*, to allow one of these things to leave your church, under any pretence whatever." They had all been borrowed for the occasion.

I grant that the poverty of many churches amply excuses the absence of all richness of ornament, silk and gold embroideries, and such-like; but what can possibly excuse want of due cleanliness, tidiness, and propriety? My seraphic Father, St. Francis, was endowed with such zeal for the most dread and holy mysteries that, although absolutely enamoured of holy poverty, he wished altars, sanctuaries, and sacristies all kept in the highest degree of neatness, and much more, of course, all that approached the adorable Sacrament. He would often occupy himself in sweeping out churches with the utmost diligence. St. Charles Borromeo, too, in giving ordination, showed himself always so precise and earnest about such things as really to astonish anyone who reads of it. To conclude, the Blessed Mother of God herself has chosen in person to enforce this propriety when, appearing to St. Bridget, she said to her, *Missa dici non debit nisi in ornamentis mundis*. (Revel. S. Brigid, 1. 6, c. 46). Mass should not be celebrated except with all that appertains to it being very clean, so as to inspire respect and devotion by the very perfection of its purity and order.

Before closing this part of the subject, it remains to say a word about the acolytes who serve at Mass. In our days this office is imposed on boys and common persons, while, in truth, the highest crowned heads are not worthy of the honor. St. Bonaventure called this an angelic office, since during the holy sacrifice many angels are in fact present, who serve God at that sacred function. (Ex. 1. 5, Spirit. grat.) The glorious St. Mechtilde once saw the soul of a poor lay brother robed in marvellous splendor, because he had exercised his zeal in serving as many Masses as he could with a perfect diligence and attention. St. Thomas Aquinas, who was the sun of the theological schools, well understanding the hidden treasure involved in this office of serving at Mass, was not satisfied after celebrating as priest unless he served at another Mass. Sir Thomas More, the celebrated lord chancellor of England, centred his chief delight in the holy employment of serving Mass; and when one day rebuked by a dignitary of the kingdom with the suggestion that King Henry would be displeased with his lowering himself thus, More replied, „My king cannot be displeased at the homage which I offer to his King." Those persons are sadly astray ----- and they are often members of religious houses ----- who require to be begged and urged to serve Mass; when, in fact, they ought to compete with each other, and almost snatch at the missal, in order to gain the honor of fulfilling a function which the very Angels and blessed ones in Heaven look upon with envy. All pains, too, should be taken to instruct properly those who serve at Mass. They should do it with lowly eyes and every trace of compunction, earnestness, and devotion. They should articulate the words distinctly, quietly, and leisurely, with voice neither so low that the priest should not hear, nor so loud as to disturb those who celebrate at adjoining altars. All children of dispositions too trivial, who are tinged with levity of demeanor, not to speak of those who could dare to joke, trifle, or make any noise, should be carefully excluded from the altar steps.

I beseech Almighty God that He would enlighten men of judgment and education to undertake this holy and honorable office! It is the noble and the wise who should set the example to others.

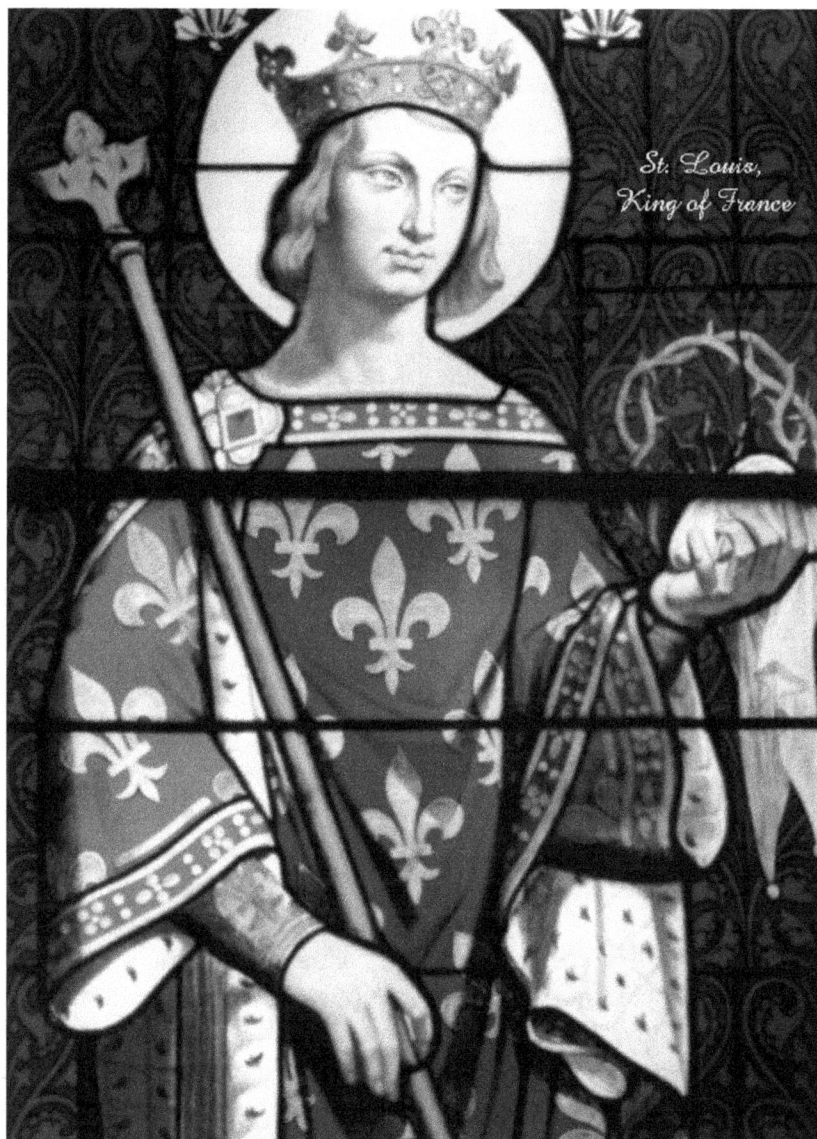

St. Louis, King of France

On Hearing Mass Daily
Part 2.: For For the Nobility and Rulers

*T*he good examples of those in high life usually move us more than the piety, however striking, of private men; the common maxim being unquestionable, *Regis ad exemplum lotus componitur orbis*, „every one follows the example of the king." And oh, what a long series of such examples might I not adduce to animate all to follow the footsteps of the great, and daily to hear holy Mass! We shall touch on a few in a passing way. Constantine the Great not only heard Mass every day in his palace, but whenever engaged in any enterprise, amid the din of war and the tumult of arms, he carried with him a portable altar, that the Divine sacrifice might be continually celebrated. Thus he continually achieved the most signal victories. The Emperor Lothaire constantly observed the same practice, in peace or in war daily hearing three Masses. The pious king of England, Henry III, in like manner, daily heard three Masses, his whole court assisting with the most exemplary devotion. *Singulis diebus tres Missas cum nota audire volebat, et plures audire cupiens, privatim celebrantibus assidue assistebat* (Matthew of Paris, His. Ang.); and therefore was he rewarded by the Lord even in things temporal, having wielded the sceptre six-and-fifty years. But, indeed, to put in evidence the piety of the English monarch, there is no need to recur to past ages; it suffices to cast our eyes on the noble soul of the most pious Queen Maria Clementina, of the exiled Stuarts, whose loss Rome has not yet ceased to deplore, and who, as she several times kindly confided to me, had placed all her pleasure in attending the Divine sacrifice, hearing, therefore, every day as many Masses as she possibly could, immovable, without cushions, without support, as if truly a statue of piety. From this attendance, so constant and so devout, there kindled in her heart a love so tenderly passionate toward Jesus in the Sacrament, that every day she would find herself present at three or four benedictions of the Most

Holy, driving quickly through the streets of Rome, so as to arrive at the different churches in time. And oh, how many tears did not this good lady shed through hunger for that Bread of Angels, a hunger so vehement as to make her languish day and night, with a heart transported constantly to the object on which she had fixed her love. Yet Almighty God permitted that her urgent instances in this particular should not be heard; and this in order to render her love heroic, so as even to make her a Martyr of Divine love, for, to the best of my belief, this frustrated desire of holy Communion hastened her death, as might be evidently gathered from the last letter which, when already sinking, she wrote to me. But what is certain is that, if frequent Communion was denied to her, the want was otherwise supplied, for that loving delight which she could not indulge in sacramental Communion she found in spiritual Communion. Not only during Mass, but many times during the day, she used to repeat her spiritual Communion with the utmost joy of heart, using exactly the form prescribed in the preceding chapter.

Now tell me: this ocular example, witnessed by ourselves, and admired in our own days by all Rome, does it not suffice to choke in their very throat the excuses of those who experience so great a difficulty in hearing holy Mass every day, and in making a spiritual Communion? If I cannot succeed in inducing you to imitate this good queen in giving up your whole heart to lively desires of receiving Jesus in the sacrament, yet I would fain have you imitate her in giving the labor of your hands, as she so often did, to provide poor churches with sacred furnishings ----- an example given indeed in Rome by many noble ladies, who make it their recreation to work with their own hands the various sacred hangings, altar linens, and such-like, for the use and ornament of churches. And, beyond Rome, may be cited the example of a princess of the highest dignity and lineage, and of not less noble virtue, who hears several Masses every morning, and very often keeps her young ladies so employed in work for the altar as to send whole chests of corporals, purificatories, and such-like to the preachers of missions, for distribution among poor churches, so that thus the divine sacrifice may be everywhere offered up to God with becoming cleanliness, decorum, and splendor. Here I must be forgiven for saying: See here, ye princes of the world, the way to make sure of Heaven. By your leave, what are you doing ----- what are you about? Why do not you open your hands, and let your liberality shine by scattering abundant alms to so many churches in such need? Do not say that the treasury is becoming empty, that imports are unproductive, and that every day the revenues diminish more and more. I shall find you a very easy way of providing for the altars of God, without prejudice to the becoming dignity of your state. Here it is, an easy one and at hand. A horse the fewer in your stables, an outrider the fewer about your carriages, a man-servant the fewer while in the country- and behold at once a large sum for aiding the necessities of many a poor parish!

You summon diets, you convoke congresses, you establish public boards, you assemble councils of war to secure your provinces; yet all does not answer; while one thought, suggestive, perhaps, of some middle course, would adjust a negotiation, and that negotiation adjusted might secure a kingdom. But that thought so advantageous, whence shall it come? From God ----- yes, understand me well ----- from God. And what the means most efficacious for obtaining it? The holy sacrifice. Hear, then, more Masses; cause, besides, many to be celebrated; provide the altars with sacred vessels, with precious vestments and furniture ----- and you will experience over you a most marvellous providence of God, which will secure your dominions, and will render you happy in time and in eternity.

Let us conclude this division with the example of St. Wenceslaus, King of Bohemia, which should at least in part be imitated by all of you. This holy king did not content himself with assisting every day at several Masses, with his knees bent on the bare pavement, nor with serving in person the celebrating priests, and this with greater humility than any cleric that has only received the lowest of minor orders; but besides this, he contributed to the sacred altars the richest jewels of his treasury, and webs of texture and embroidery the most precious in the royal wardrobes. He was, further, in the habit of making with his own hands the altar-bread which was to be used for the holy sacrifice; and with this view, without any regard to the royal dignity, he applied those hands, born to wield the sceptre, in cultivating a field, in directing the plough, in sowing the seed, and in reaping the harvest. Then he ground the grain, separated the finer flour for the oven, and made the breads which should afterward be Consecrated; and these he presented, with the lowliest reverence, to the priests, to be converted into the most Divine Body of the Saviour. O hands worthy to have held the sceptre of this globe! And did other kings despise him for this? Far from it. Almighty God led the Emperor Otho I to conceive for this holy king an unparalleled regard, so far as to grant him the right to quarter in his arms the imperial device (an eagle sable in an argent field), a favor not extended to any other prince. Thus God, by means of the emperor, rewarded with temporal honors the great devotion of Wenceslaus toward the Divine sacrifice. But much more was he rewarded by the King of Heaven when, by means of a most glorious Martyrdom, there was granted to him a crown of eternal glory: and thus we behold him, through his passionate tenderness for holy Mass, doubly crowned, in this and in the other world. Reflect and resolve.

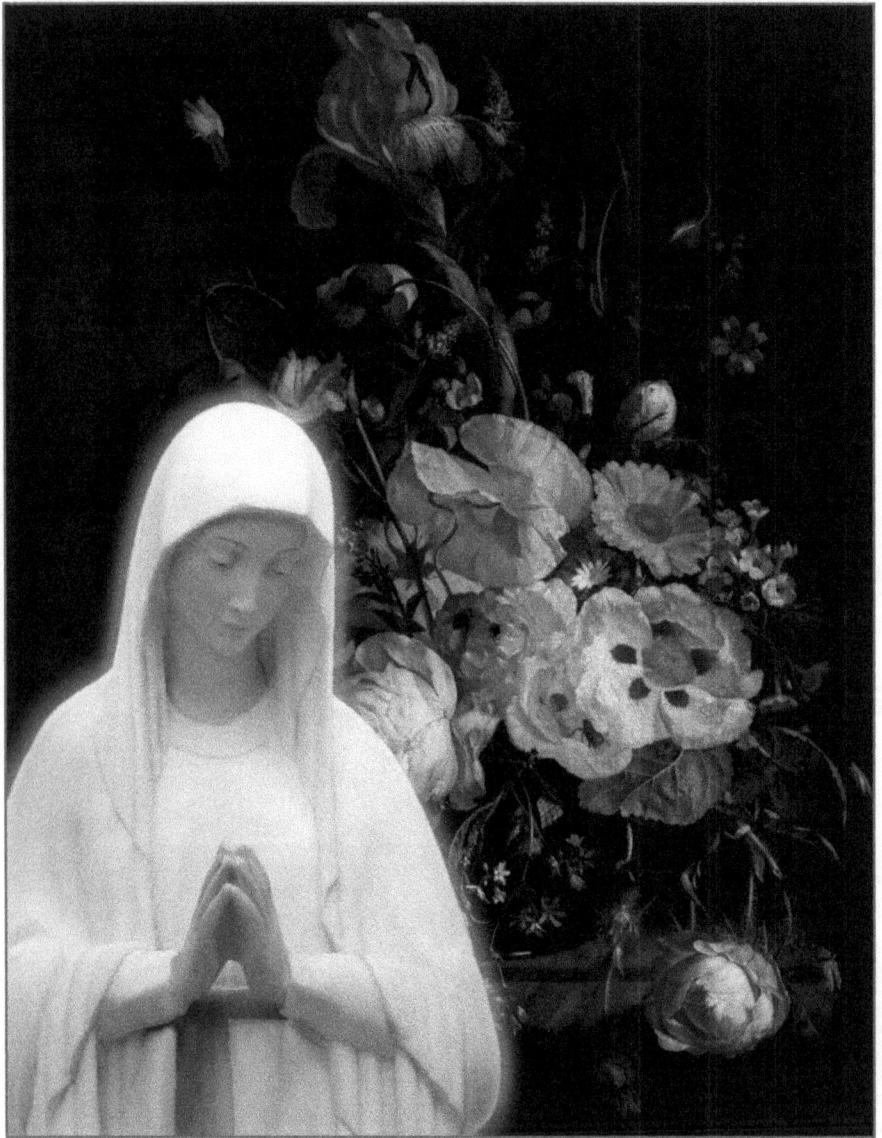

On Hearing Mass Daily
Part 3.: Ladies Dress

*A*ady who enters church decked out with various ornaments is apt to attract attention, and perhaps, though God forbid it, to withdraw hearts from the worship of God. It is needless to adduce examples to encourage ladies to hear holy Mass every day. Truly they are but too well inclined to frequent churches, and the thing in point is to make them understand with what modesty and reverence they ought to demean themselves in the house of God, and more particularly when the holy sacrifice is being celebrated; since, however much many ladies edify me, appearing as they do before the altars in simple dress, without variety of color, without anything elaborate or curious, I am as much scandalized, on the other hand, by those vain trifling creatures who, arrayed in the fashion of the hour, and with an air caught as it were from the theatre, almost seem as if they would be the goddesses of some temple. The Blessed Ivetta, herself a noble Flemish lady, had once a wonderful vision in church. Such a one as I have mentioned was not far distant from her during holy Mass, magnificently dressed, and the Saint was enlightened to see the disposition of her heart, and the vain, worldly, and even impure thoughts which came and went freely through her mind without any check. And all the while she perceived that there were evil spirits close to this self-complacent woman of fashion, who would at times seem to touch her lace or her ribbons as objects of which they had a care. The lady approached the altar-rails for holy Communion; the priest descended the steps, the adorable Sacrament in his hand, when, lo, the Saviour separated Himself from the sacred particle, and ascending heavenward, disappeared, refusing to enter the mouth of one so wretched as to carry her vanity into His very presence and there complacently to dwell on thoughts of sin. The Saint was made clearly to understand that the evil spirits who were near her found in her luxury and vanity of dress something congenial to their minds and easy instruments for her ruin, and that the Saviour refused to be given to her because of her sinful dispositions. *Quoniam in malevolam animam non introibit sapientia, nec habitabit in corpore subdito peccatis,* „For wisdom will not enter into a malicious soul, nor dwell in a body subject to sins" (Wis. i. 4).

But you will say to me that you are not of the number of those so corrupt and lost; and I believe you ----- with all frankness I believe you: but yet all that finery, those perfumes, that search after effect; that studious calculation of means to heighten every good feature of face, figure, or complexion; that pride of splendor and outlay; how shall these things be sternly enough denounced? Do you not, so far as you can, degrade the house of God; do you not rob Christ of honor, by casting more or less of distraction by your demeanor and your finery? Ah, enter into your own hearts, and resolve to imitate St. Elizabeth of Hungary ----- a Saint, a queen, who would go with all royal pomp to holy Mass, but on entering church would take the crown from her head, the jewels from her fingers, and, despoiled of all ornament, would remain covered with a veil, so modest in deportment that she was never seen to direct a glance in any direction but the altar. This so pleased Almighty God that He chose to make His satisfaction apparent to all; for once, during Mass, the Saint was so glorified with Divine splendor that the eyes which looked on her were dazzled, and she seemed to all as it were an angel of paradise. Make use of this noble example, and be assured you will thus become pleasing to God and to man, and your share in the divine sacrifice will be of the highest profit to you in this life and in the next.

FOR WOMEN IN GENERAL

Great, indeed, is the benefit to be derived from holy Mass, as has been shown in the preceding instances; but very often it is not befitting for all women to go to church on week days. You who nurse a child, or are obliged by motives, whether of virtue or of charity, to assist the sick, or you who have a perverse husband, who forbids you to leave the house, must not be troubled about it, or, what would be worse, disobey; for though holy Mass is indeed a thing most holy and, as we have shown, of the utmost benefit, yet, for all this, obedience and the denial of your own will are better in your case. Nay, for your consolation be it known to you that by such obedience you acquire double grace and merit, since the goodness of God in such a case will not only reward your obedience, but will look on you as having attended Mass, graciously accepting your good intention. By disobedience, on the contrary, you would lose the one and the other merit, showing yourself to have more pleasure in your own will than in that of God, Who expressly declares in the page of Holy Writ that *Melior est obedientia quam victimae* (1 Kings xv. 22). God is more pleased with obedience than with Masses and sacrifices not of precept. But what if you should go to Mass in such circumstances, only to meet acquaintances with whom to chat, or in such a spirit as to indulge in voluntary distractions, and thus cause you to return home empty-handed as to all benefit? So it was with a country woman who lived in a village at some little distance from church. (Heur, in Mag. Spec. Exem. d. 10 Ex. 28.) Tn order to win some great favor or another which she desired of Almighty God, she determined and engaged to herself that she would hear a great number of Masses in the course of the year. And so, whenever she heard the bell of invitation to the holy sacrifice ring from any neighboring country church, she would immediately interrupt her occupations and make hastily off, even through rain or snow, without taking at all into account the inclemency of the weather. When again at home she would, in order to keep count of the Masses so as to complete the number precisely, slip a bean into a box through a small slit like that in money-boxes or those used for voting, so that it seemed a perfectly secure repository. When the year had flown, confident of having fulfilled her vow, of having presented a great offering of homage to God, and of having acquired no little merit, she went to open the little case, where, of all the beans she had deposited, she found one only. Confounded and amazed beyond measure, she quite took it to heart, and turning to God, she said with tears: „O Lord, how is it that so many Masses at which I have assisted, I only find the record of one? Nor have I ever failed to be present, even at the very greatest inconvenience, never fearing adverse weather, but hurrying through rain or hail, and in spite of whatever seemed to oppose me." Then Almighty God inspired her to go and consult a wise and pious priest, who asked her in what spirit she had pursued her devotion, her demeanor on the way to, and the affections with which she had assisted at the sacrifice. To all which she had to acknowledge that on the way to church she had always been thinking about her affairs, or chatting in a light and jocular style; and that, while assisting at the Divine mysteries, she had passed much of the time in whispering with some friend or neighbor, or had occupied her mind with domestic cares. „Behold the cause," exclaimed the priest, „of so many Masses being lost. Chatting, idle curiosity, and voluntary distractions have taken away all your merit. Either the devil has taken your tokens as a record against you, or your angel has carried them off, that you might see how good works are lost if not done in the right way and the right spirit. But be sure you return thanks to God that one at least seems to have been well heard and has remained profitable to you." Now make a serious reflection, and say to yourself: Who knows how many out of all the Masses heard during my life, may have been accepted by God and agreeable to Him? What says conscience? If it seems that but few have been profitable to you in the sight of God, apply the remedy in a true and thorough spirit of amendment for the future. But if, which God forbid, you have been one of those unfortunates who levy recruits for hell, dragging souls down to it even in church, listen to the following frightful incident, and tremble. It is handed down in a book called „Dormisicuro," as a well-founded story, that a woman, for a long time suffering deep poverty, wandered about in a sort of despair through solitary places, and that there, in some way or other, an evil spirit intimated to her that if she had conducted herself in church as some did, entertaining those near with idle whisperings and useless and impertinent talk, he would have befriended her and made her better off. The miserable woman accepted the bargain thus suggested, applied herself to the miserable and devilish work, and succeeded marvellously; for whoever happened to be placed beside her found it impossible to attend devoutly to Mass or other Divine functions, so constant were her observations or questions, and so many the little methods of interruption which she applied. But no long time passed before she felt the avenging hand of God. One morning there occurred a violent tempest, and a thunderbolt fell among the crowd, which slew her alone, reducing her to ashes. Learn, then, at another's cost, and avoid those who with idle talk, and with so much irreverence in church, make themselves truly the servants of Satan; spurn them if you do not yourselves wish to incur the wrath of God.

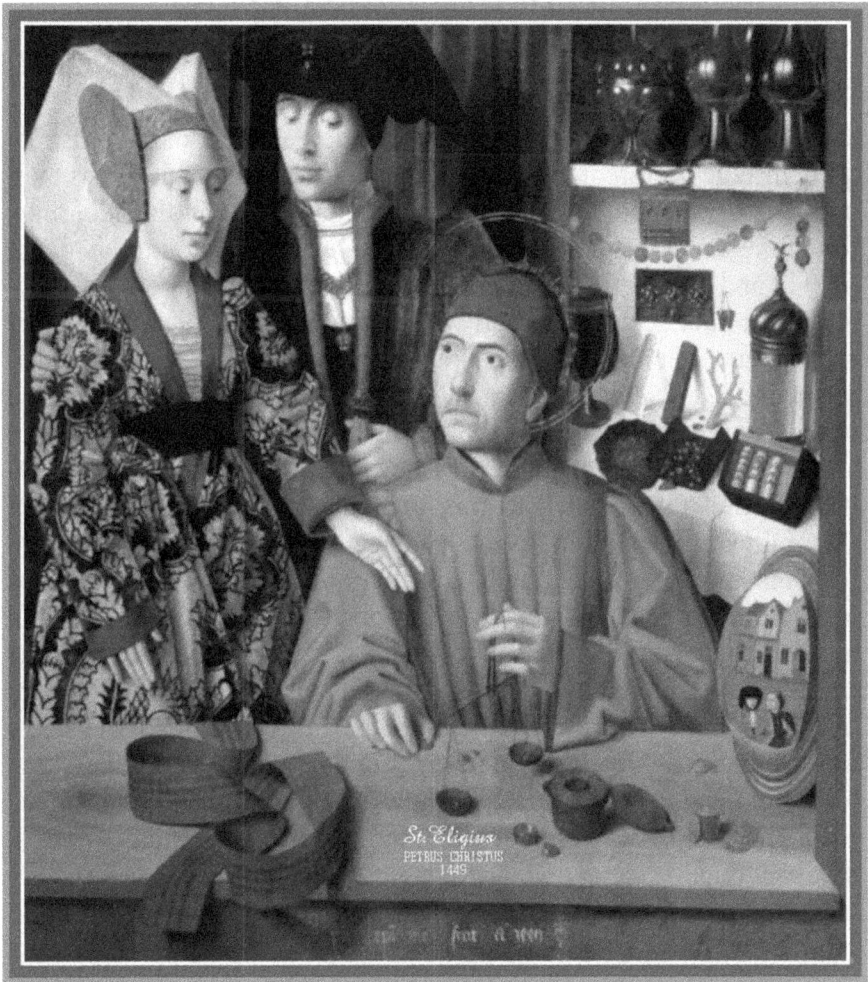

St. Eligius by Petrus Christus, 1449

On Hearing Mass Daily
Part 4.: For Tradesmen and Artisans

*T*he idol of our times is self-interest, and, alas, how many prostrate themselves before it, offering to it at all times and in all places their undivided homage! And thence it comes that, pursuing this idol, they forget the true God, and so come to plunge themselves into an abyss of evil, and a perpetual destitution of all true good; whereas, the holy Royal Prophet declares that all who in the first place seek God shall not encounter any evil, but shall abound in all good. *Inquirentes Dominum non deficient omni bono* (Ps. xxxiii. 11). This is amply verified in those who, before applying to their business, manage first to assist at holy Mass, as the adventure which is told of certain traders of Gubbio well illustrates. They had gone to a public fair held in the town of Cisternino, and having made a clearance of their wares, two of them began to speak of going, and fixed to start the next day at dawn, so as to arrive by evening in their own neighborhood. But the third would not consent to start then, and protested that, next day being Sunday, he could never think of commencing a journey without having first heard holy Mass; that then, after a little food, they might take their departure more to their satisfaction, and that, should they not succeed in getting to Gubbio that evening, there was no want of comfortable inns on the road. His companions did not yield to this wise and salutory counsel, but, bent on arriving at home next night, they answered that Almighty God would have compassion on them if they lost Mass for once. So on Sunday morning before dawn, without ever entering church, they took their way on horseback toward home. They arrived near the river Corfuone. By the violent rain which had fallen during the night it was now excessively swollen, and the current beating strongly against the wooden bridge had somewhat shaken and weakened it. They advanced upon it with their horses, and no sooner had they reached the middle than a still further rise and furious rush of the flood broke down and swept away the whole structure. The two unhappy traders were, of course, plunged with their horses into the river and drowned, losing at once their money, their goods, their lives, and almost certainly their souls. At the sound of the crash, and sight of the havoc, the peasants ran to the spot, and contrived with hooks to draw the corpses out, which they then left stretched out on the bank, in order that, if possible, they might be recognized and obtain burial. Soon after, the third trader, who had been detained by his wish to satisfy the precept of attending Mass, and who had then taken to the road with joyful alacrity, came up to the river and beheld the two bodies on the bank. Drawing up to observe them, he instantly recognized his two companions, and heard from the bystanders all the miserable catastrophe with the utmost agitation of spirit. Then he lifted his hands to Heaven, returning thanks to the Most High, Who had so mercifully preserved him; and he blessed a thousand times the hour in which he assisted at the Holy Sacrifice, clearly recognizing the source of his safety. When again at home, he announced the sad intelligence, got the relations to procure proper interment for the departed, and stirred up among all a lively desire of daily attendance at holy Mass. (Lohner. tom. 2, tit. 64.)

O accursed avarice! ----- let me give vent to what I feel ----- accursed passion, that cuttest off the heart from God, and takest away, as it were, from us the very faculty of free will, so far as regards the power of attending to the great business of eternal salvation!

That the avaricious may enter into themselves, I will illustrate my meaning by an example from Holy Scripture. Samson, you are aware, was bound in vain even with the sinews of oxen, and with fresh ropes never before used. At last he informed his treacherous wife that the secret of his strength lay hid in the locks of his hair; and so no sooner were they cut off than he lost all his wonderful strength, fell into the power of the Philistines, was made blind by them, and condemned to work a mill. Now, what was the chief and prime error of Samson? Was it, perhaps, in allowing himself to be so securely bound? That was not his error. The evil lay in telling the secret of his strength, and thus allowing the loss of his mysterious locks, which once gone, he was no longer himself. Now, a man engaged in trade doubtless permits himself to be bound by a thousand ties of traffic, of accounts, of exchange, and so on. Does the deadly peril of avarice consist in all this? No, not in all this. The danger lies in cutting off the locks of hair. Let me explain. Suppose a man in trade to have never so great a pressure of business, but hearing betimes every morning the bells that call to Mass, says to himself, „Business, wait a little; have patience; let us get our Mass safely settled:" such a man is Samson bound but not shorn ----- bound by the thousand cords of business, but not shorn of the secret source of strength. Another is also caught in a multitude of cords: workmen to pay, accounts to clear, letters to write, correspondents with whom to negotiate: one man expects an answer, another his money. Alas, what a labyrinth of bonds! No matter, Sunday at last comes round, or the festival of some Saint, his patron perhaps; he breaks loose from all, and goes with devotion to hear some Masses and offer up his prayers. This man also is a Samson bound but not shorn; for, amid all his affairs, he never loses sight of the great business of eternal salvation. But attend to me now: if you are bound by a thousand ties of interest, without vigor to snap them through, if you fail to come forth at the proper time, and cease firmly to frequent the Sacraments and the holy sacrifice, then woe to you; then are you both bound and shorn. In this case, though your gains be just, yet at such a cost they are sinful; there is within you a coarse and horrid avarice, which will treat you as Samson was treated, until, at last, as with Samson, the roof overhead shall fall in upon you. Then quae parasti cujus erunt? ----- „whose shall those things be which thou hast provided?" (St. Luke xii. 20)

But you are thinking that the avaricious will never listen except to a tune in their own key. Well, then, be it so. Get rich, gather up, make profit. What is the surest way? I will show you: daily hear holy Mass with thorough devotion. It is plainly seen in the case of two artisans whom I could point out. Both pursue the same trade; one is burdened with a family: wife, children, grandchildren; the other is alone with his wife. The first has brought up his family in great comfort and even style, and all his transactions turned out wonderfully. Customers at his shop, and sales dispatched. So he has gone on, till he finds himself putting by every year a good round sum, to serve in time for marriage-portions for his daughters. The other, who is without children, at one time got little employment, was half famished, and was, in short, a ruined man. One day he said confidentially to his neighbor, „How is it you do? In your home there rains down every blessing of God; while I, poor wretch, cannot hold up my head, and all sorts of calamities light on my house." „I will tell you," said his neighbor; „tomorrow morning I shall be with you, and I will point out the place from which I draw so much." Next morning he took him to church to hear Mass, and then led him back to his workshop; and so two or three different times, till at last the poor man said, „If nothing else is wanted than to go to church to hear Mass, I know the way well enough, without putting you to inconvenience." „Just so," said the other; „hear holy Mass, my friend, with devotion, every day, and you will see a change on the face of your fortune." And, in fact, so it was. Beginning to hear holy Mass every morning, he became well provided with work, shortly paid his debts, and put his house once more in capital condition. (Sar. in Vito S. Joan. Eleem.) Trust to the words of the Gospel. And if you do so, how can you doubt the fact? Does it not say clearly, *Quaerite primum regnum Dei . . . et haec omnia adjicientur vobis?* „Seek first the kingdom of God, and all these things shall be added unto you." (St. Matt. vi. 33.) Make but the trial for a year; hear holy Mass every morning with true earnest devotion for one year, and if your temporal interests do not take a better turn, lay the blame on me. But there is little fear of that; you will rather have many reasons to thank me.

On Hearing Mass Daily
Part 5.: For Laborers

*T*he Apostle St. Paul says that he who does not duly provide for and take care of his family is worse than an infidel. *Si quis suorum, et maxime domesticorum curam non habet, fidem negavit, et est infideli deterior* (1 Tim. v. 8). This is to be understood, not only of their bodies, but much rather of their souls; so that if it would be a great impiety to leave one's household in want of corporal food, a much greater depth of unfaithfulness must it be to deprive them of spiritual aliment, and, especially, of the utmost facility for daily hearing holy Mass ----- the loss of which can never be compensated by any master, however rich and powerful he may be. When God established with Abraham the great covenant, He commanded that not he alone should be circumcised, but also all his servants and all his slaves, *Tam vernaculus, quam emptitius circumcidetur* (Gen. xvii. 12), an evident sign that the good Christian ought not to be content with going by himself to Divine worship, and specially to holy Mass, but ought to take pains to induce all his servants, and all portions of his family, to give themselves to the worship of God. This hallowed household rule was practised in all its propriety and gracefulness by St. Elzear, Count of Ariano, who, among many good regulations which he gave to his family, made this the first, that all in his employ should every morning hear holy Mass.

Men-servants, women-servants, pages, grooms: he made a point of seeing them all at Mass ----- a most holy custom, and one practised, thank God, by many men of rank, and by all the ecclesiastical dignitaries of Rome. These every morning hear holy Mass, and make all their retinue and servants assist also. Nor ought any one to fancy that this amount of time occupied by your servant in hearing holy Mass is time lost. Well shall it be recompensed by God.

St. Isidore was a poor farm-laborer, but one who never missed hearing holy Mass every morning; and Almighty God, in order to show him how pleased He was with his devotion, once when he was assisting at Mass, caused his field to be ploughed for him by the concealed service of angels. It is true that God may not work such striking miracles for you, but in how many other ways may He not repay your piety? You may draw your own conclusions from that which I believe to have happened to a poor working-man. He was a vine-dresser, who maintained his family by the sweat of his brow. Every day, before going to his work, he was in the habit of being present at the holy sacrifice of the Mass. One morning having gone betimes to the spot appointed for day-laborers seeking hire, he stood waiting for some proprietor to select and conduct him to his day's work. At length hearing the sound of the bell, he betook himself, according to his custom, to church, there to offer his prayers. That Mass ended, there then commenced a second; and, stimulated by his devotion, he heard this other Mass also. When he returned to the accustomed place, he found it solitary, every one being already hired by various proprietors in the neighborhood; so the good man, much cast down, returned toward his house; but in the way encountered a wealthy citizen, who, struck with the clouds of grief on his brow, asked whence arose his sorrow. „What would you have?" said the poor fellow. „This morning, in order not to lose Mass, I have lost my day's hire." „Give yourself no trouble about that," said the rich citizen, „go to church, hear another Mass for my intention, and this evening I will pay you a day's hire." The poor man went and heard all the Masses celebrated that day, and in the evening went to receive his wage, which consisted of twelve *soldi*, the usual pay of day-laborers in that district. He was going contentedly home, when he met an unknown personage (as I conceive, the Saviour of the world Himself) who asked what reward he had obtained for a day so well employed. And on hearing the reply, He said, „What! so little for work so meritorious? Go back to the rich man, and tell him that if he do not increase the gift, his affairs shall all go wrong." This simple soul took the message to the citizen, who gave him five pieces more and bade him go in peace. The poor man was quite satisfied with his increase, but Jesus was not satisfied! „Return," said the unknown counsellor, „return to the niggardly man, and tell him that if he do not increase your reward, he may look for a dreadful disaster." Again he went with a demeanor of timid respect, and with hesitating utterance and low voice, delivered his message. Then the rich man, deeply struck, and moved interiorly by God, went so far as to give him a hundred *soldi*, with some clothing quite good and new. (Nicol. Lag. tract. 6, d. 10, de Mis. G. 100.)

No doubt you admire with reason Divine Providence thus interposing in behalf of this poor vine-dresser, because of the pious devotion with which he had always assisted at the holy sacrifice. But much more worthy of admiration is the favor which the Sovereign Mercy thus contrived to exercise toward the rich man; for the following night the Saviour appeared to him in sleep, and related to him that, through the Masses heard for him by his poor neighbor, He had remitted the sudden death which had been destined that very night to plunge him into Hell. At this terrific announcement, he awoke, and full of horror for his evil ways, he became most devout toward holy Mass, at which he continued to assist every morning, and caused also many to be celebrated every day in different churches, till at last, after a virtuous life, he ended his days by a happy death.

See now how gracious is God's bounty toward those who prove devout lovers of the holy sacrifice of Mass. Ah, hasten then, my poor friends, hasten to Mass, and be very sure that by this one exercise of devotion you shall find consolation amid all your trials.

Christ Holding a Crown by Taddeo Di Bartolo, c. 1405

On Hearing Mass Daily
Part 6.: A Solemn Warning

Two Doctors of the Church, the angelic St. Thomas and the seraphic St. Bonaventure, teach, in conformity with the foregoing instruction, that the thrice-holy sacrifice of Mass is of infinite value, both by reason of the Victim Who is offered, namely, the Body, Blood, Soul, and Divinity of Jesus Christ Our Lord, and also by reason of the primary Offerer, Who is no other than the same Jesus Himself. Yet by how many is it so little valued that they postpone the inestimable treasure to every vile and petty interest! This little work is drawn up for the express purpose that all who shall deign to read it may remain enlightened for all time to come, and may arrive at something like a due conception of a pearl that is beyond all price. And if hitherto this holy sacrifice has been to them a hidden treasure, now that its infinite value has been pointed out, may they resolve to possess it by a daily share in the priestly act! To promote this end, I narrate the following dreadful incident, which shall serve for the seal to all my words.

Aeneas Silvius, afterward Pius II, recounts how in a city in Germany there lived a person of distinction, the principal inhabitant of the place, who had fallen into great difficulties, and had withdrawn into a country house, with a view to economy. There, overwhelmed by melancholy, he was on the verge of despair. The enemy saw this, and the temptation which he constantly instilled was the longing to slip a cord about his neck, and so have done with life. A dry tree, said the Evil One, is good for nothing but the hatchet. In this conflict of grief and temptations, the nobleman had recourse to a holy confessor, who gave him this good advice: „Do not let one day pass without hearing holy Mass, and have no fear." He accepted the advice, and promptly began to put it into execution; and in order to make sure of never losing holy Mass, he gave a salary to a chaplain, who, at his request, constantly offered the adorable sacrifice, at which he took care to assist every morning with pious devotion. But it happened that one day his chaplain went at an early hour to a neighboring village, to assist a young priest, who was about to celebrate his first Mass. The devout nobleman, fearing that he would that day be deprived of the sacrifice, hastened to the same village, in order to be present at it. On the way he met a peasant, who told him that he might as well turn back, because the last Mass was ended. Much disturbed in mind, the nobleman began even to shed tears. „Alas! what shall I do?" he kept repeating. „What shall I make of myself today? Perhaps it may be the last of my poor life." The countryman was astonished to see him so much agitated; and being himself a man careless of his soul, he exclaimed, „Pray, do not weep, my lord, do not weep; for my part, if it is a thing that can be done, I don't a bit mind selling you my share in today's Mass. Give me that good cloak off your back, and, for aught I care, my Mass is yours this moment." The nobleman agreed gladly to the strange proposal, thinking he would take the chance of possibly getting something by it, at least for his good intentions' sake, and so, handing over his cloak, he pursued his path toward church. There he offered a short prayer; and on his return, had hardly got to the place where the bargain had been struck, when he saw the miserable man who had conceived the profane and extragavant design of selling his Mass hanging by the neck from an oak, and already dead, like another Judas. In fact, the temptation to self-destruction had passed into the unhappy peasant, who had voluntarily deprived himself of the aid which he might have had from the sacrifice, and designedly left himself powerless to resist the malignant suggestions of the devil. Then the worthy nobleman began to perceive how effectual was the remedy which his confessor had advised, and was from that moment confirmed in his holy determination daily to assist at the Divine mysteries.

I should wish you to extract from an incident so mournful a due perception of two points of great importance: first, how horrible is the excessive ignorance of some Christians who, not recognizing the immense preciousness of holy Mass, come to treat it as a matter of vulgar purchase for filthy lucre. Thence, sometimes, the indecent language with which such persons will address a priest; as, for instance, „May I pay for a Mass this morning?" Pay for Mass! And where will you find capital for that? What is the equivalent for a Mass, when one unbloody sacrifice of Christ outweighs in value the whole of paradise itself? Such ignorance is intolerable. The trifle you give to the priest is a gift toward his daily support, not in any sense the payment of so much purchase-money, for holy Mass is a treasure without price. It is true that in this little work I have exhorted you to hear holy Mass every day, and cause it to be celebrated as often as you can; and who knows, therefore, whether the devil may not have put into your head the suspicion that monks exhort you with fine and specious arguments to get Masses celebrated, but that all is not gold that glitters; that perhaps they seek their own gain, under the show of zeal, and that when you peep behind the mask you will, very likely, find that all is said for their own interests. Oh, how much you would deceive yourselves if thus you thought! I thank God, Who has caused me to embrace a religious institute in which is professed the strictest and most perfect poverty, where no alms are received for Mass, and where no sum, however great, would be looked at on such an occasion, for we say all our Masses with no other intention than that which Christ had on the cross when He offered to the Eternal Father that first sacrifice on Calvary. Therefore, if anyone may speak out clearly on this subject, without any fear of reproval, it is I, who seek merely your good; as I do in all the other matters touched on in this little book, which now at its close I sum up afresh. Hear many Masses, I beseech you; hear many; cause many to be celebrated; get as many as you can. Make sure of this great treasure, which will be to you indeed a treasure both in this world and the next.

The second point to be extracted and stored up out of the incident now narrated is the efficacy of holy Mass for winning every benefit from on high, for procuring exemption or escape from every evil, and particularly for obtaining or reinvigorating our spiritual energies, so as to insure victory over all temptations. Let me, then, repeat: to Mass, I beseech of you; to Mass, if you want to triumph over your soul's enemies, and to behold all Hell cast down and trampled under your feet.

One single counsel remains to be repeated, one applicable alike to clergy and seculars, which is, that to obtain in great abundance the fruits of holy Mass, you must hear it with the deepest devotion. I have struck at this nail several times in the course of my little book, but now just at the close, I must beat at it with still more vigor. When at Mass, keep deeply engaged in devotion; and, if you like, make use of this book, putting it in practice with all the exactitude prescribed in the second chapter. I boldly refer you to experience as your master; for in a short time you will be conscious of a sensible change in your heart, and you will, so to speak, be able to touch with your very hand the great blessing which you will carry at your heart.

And for you, O priests, tremble before the justice of God if, either by excessive haste or irreverent negligence, you transgress the rules of the sacred ceremoines, if you hurry out your words, or confuse the different acts, and, in short, bustle slipshod through your Mass. Reflect that then you consecrate, you touch, you receive, the Son of the Most High; nor are you blameless in regard to each the very slightest cere-mony which you either leave out or perform more or less imperfectly. Such is the teaching of the most learned Suarez, when he treats of the question, *Vel unius caerimoniae omissio culpae reatum inducit* (T. 5, in 3 part. dist. 85. lect. 2). Whence that oracle of Spain, [St.] John of Avila, was always firmly of opinion that the Eternal Judge will, in the case of priests, make, before every thing else, a most rigorous scrutiny into all the Masses they have celebrated. Thus when on one occasion a young priest had departed to the other world, just as he had barely finished his first Mass, the holy man, hearing of his death, heaved a sigh, and asked, „Had he ever offered Mass?" And when they told of his happy fate in dying so soon as his first Mass was celebrated, „Ah," he resumed, „he has much to thank God for if he has once celebrated Mass!" But you and I, who have celebrated so many, how shall we pass before the tribunal of God? Let us, then, make the holy resolution to re-study (at latest in our first spiritual retreat) all the rubrics of the Missal, and all the sacred ceremonial, so as to celebrate for the future with all the exactness possible. It is my hope that if we priests shall generally celebrate with serious and devout exterior composure, and, what is far more, with thorough interior fervor of soul, the laity will return to daily hearing of holy Mass, and to hearing it with deepest de-votion. Thus we shall have the joy of beholding renewed in the Chris-tians of our time all the fervor of the first believers of God's Church, and thus will our most gracious and Almighty God be supremely ho-nored and glorified ------ -the sole and single aim of this poor work.

Reader, say for me one „HAIL MARY."

St. Leonard is in Heaven, and needs no prayers: the charitable reader will perhaps say the „Hail Mary" for him who has translated these pages.

The Holy Eucharist by Juan De Juanes, c. 1560

Chapter 4

Easy Method of Attending Holy Mass with Profit

PRAYERS BEFORE AND DURING HOLY MASS

A Prayer of most humble Devotion to the Holy Spirit, to be offered before hearing Holy Mass, in order to implore His aid

Come, O Holy Spirit, and with Thy most holy grace gather together, I beseech of Thee, all the faculties and all the affections of my soul, so that, with devout attention and with my whole heart, I may be able to attend this holy Mass, and obtain thereby those benefits for which, albeit unworthy, I ardently hope, to the greater glory of God and the benefit of my own soul, through the goodness and compassion of the same my Lord and God. Amen. Prayer while the Priest says the Confiteor O my most loving Saviour, Who, when weighed down with faintness and grief of heart, in the garden of Gethsemane, didst turn in fervent prayer to the Eternal Father, while the drops of Thy bloody sweat ran down profusely to the ground; grant me the grace that, in memory of Thy most holy Passion, I may, at least, shed abundant tears of grief and contrition, as Thou Thy bloody sweat of agony that night. Amen.

Prayer when the Priest begins the Introit

O my most benign and gentle Saviour, Who, when led like a malefactor before Annas, didst receive from the fierce Jews those cruel blows, grant that, in imitation of Thee, I also may receive with willingness the affronts of my enemies, and bear up under all the troubles and temptations of this treacherous world. Amen.

Prayer while the Priest repeats the Kyrie Eleison.

O my Lord Jesus Christ, Who in the house of Caiphas wast three times basely denied by Peter, chief of Thy apostles; I humbly pray Thee, make me ever to shun wicked companions, so that I may never, by following them, and through my own grievous sinfulness and imperfection, be led away from Thee and Thine infinite goodness. Amen.

Prayer while the Priest reads the Epistle

O my most compassionate Saviour, Who, being conducted to Pilate's house by the Jews, with every kind of outrage, wast unjustly accused by false witnesses in His presence; teach me, I pray thee, to fly all the snares of the wicked; and enable me, amid the constant practice of good works, ever sincerely and openly to profess Thy holy Catholic Faith, till the latest moment of my life. Amen.

Prayer while the Priest reads the Gospel

O my most merciful Lord, Who, when sent back by Herod to Pilate, wast the occasion of their reconciliation, grant to me such strength that I may never fear the devices of the wicked, but rather obtain from persecutions and trials such benefit that, even in the midst of them, my heart may never be troubled, but ever grow more and more conformed, in and by all things, to Thy most holy will. Amen.

Prayer while the Priest offers the Sacrifice

My Lord Jesus Christ, Who, to satisfy the justice of the Eternal Father for my sins, didst freely choose to be bound to the column, and under so many stripes to scatter Thy most Precious Blood; grant me the grace to cleanse my soul of the hideous stains of sin in those ruddy streams, so that I may offer it all fresh and pure, in union with Thy merits, to the Eternal Father. Amen.

Prayer while the Priest washes his Fingers

O my most compassionate Saviour, O Son of the living God, Who, when declared innocent by Pilate Thy judge, didst patiently bear the tumult and the eager cries of the Jews, in their bitter malice against Thee; grant me the grace to lead a life truly innocent amid the stormy waves of this world, and present only the resistance of patient charity to the outrages and attacks of enemies. Amen.

Prayer while the Priest says the Preface

O my most sweet and gentle Saviour, Who didst receive from Pilate the unjust sentence to die ignominiously on the cross, grant me the grace that when I shall arrive at the last hour of my life, I may, through love of Thee, feel no fear when my sentence of death, however painful, has at last to be put in force; but that I may sigh out my soul in the embrace of Thy most sacred arms. Amen.

Prayer while the Priest prays for the Living

O my most compassionate Saviour, Who didst will, for the redemption of the world, to carry the heavy Cross upon Thy shoulders, even to Mount Calvary, grant me the grace that following Thy example, I may willingly embrace the cross of the mortifications and trials of this world, and bear it patiently, for love of Thee, even unto death. Amen.

Prayer while the Priest elevates the Host

O my most merciful Saviour, Who, after being shamefully nailed to the Cross by the hands of wicked men, wast lifted up from the ground upon it; uplift, I beseech Thee, by the excess of Thine infinite compassion, my poor heart above all earthly passions and cares, so as to give my mind to nothing but thoughts of Thy most holy Passion, of my own death, and of the eternal things of Heaven. Amen.

Prayer while the Priest elevates the Chalice

My Lord Jesus Christ, Who didst will that the true fountain of all graces should be Thy Blood gushing over us from Thy most Sacred Wounds, cause me always, when suddenly assailed by evil thoughts, to have recourse to the power and efficacy of these most sacred wounds, and to draw from them my certain remedy, so as ever to rise victorious over temptation during my whole life. Amen.

Prayer while the Priest intercedes for the Departed

My most gracious Saviour, Who, while fixed in anguish on the Cross, didst pray to the Eternal Father for the salvation of all the human race, for those even who crucified Thee; inflame my heart with the heavenly fire of a most ardent love, so that in all time coming, taught by Thy example, I may learn tenderly to love my neighbor and to do good even to mine enemies. Amen.

Prayer while the Priest recites the Our Father

My Lord Jesus Christ, Who, just before Thy death of most bitter anguish, didst recommend Thy Mother, the most Blessed Virgin, to St. John, and then the same John I to her; be pleased ever to accept my body and soul, so that, by means of Thy most holy help, I may quickly advance in the way of the Spirit and of perfection. Amen.

Prayer while the Priest puts into the Chalice a portion of the Host

O my most merciful Saviour, Who, descending after death, didst rejoice with Thy Divine presence the poor expectant Souls of the patriarchs, cause, I beseech Thee, by the virtue of Thy most Precious Blood, and of Thy most holy Passion, to descend upon all the Souls suffering in Purgatory, so that, freed from these their dreadful pains, they may be admitted to enjoy the eternal glory of Heaven. Amen.

Prayer while the Priest says the Agnus Dei

My Lord Jesus Christ, since many of the Jews recognized their transgressions, and wept for their sins, at the cruel sight of Thy most bitter death, grant me the grace, through the merits of that death, that I, too, may bitterly weep and lament for my sins. Amen.

Prayer while the Priest receives the most holy Communion

My most gracious Lord, Who, for the redemption of the whole human race, didst permit Thy most Precious Body to be placed at burial in a new sepulchre, grant me the grace that my heart may be so made new as to be ready for Thee to enter therein. Amen.

Prayer while the Priest gives his Blessing to the People

O my Lord, most loving and most worthy to be loved, Who, while Thy disciples were all intently given to prayer, didst send down from Heaven the Holy Spirit to console them; purify, I beseech Thee, my heart with Thy most holy grace, so that the Holy Spirit, finding in it a pleasing abode, may dwell therein, and so enrich the poverty of my soul. Amen.

The Return of the Prodigal Son by Murillo, 1660

Chapter 5

Devout Exercises of Preparation and Thanksgiving for Confession and Holy Communion

Soul, that dost belong to God, read and consider these devout exercises. The more you read and make your own these good and fervent thoughts, the more will you please Jesus, and the greater your reward in the life eternal. If at the first sentence you find yourself struck with devotion and compunction, pass no farther on, but rest where God hath begun to draw and work upon you.

When circumstances prevent your communicating sacramentally, fail not to do so spiritually, breathing out your love to Jesus, and desiring to receive Jesus in the Sacrament. Prepare yourself for this spiritual Communion by the following devout acts, affections, and exercises.

Exercises for Confession

Weep, O my soul, for all your sins; detest your guilt beyond every form of calamity; and do so with the purpose of Confession: for by your sins you have offended God your Father; you have offended God your Creator; you have offended your God Who hath never injured you; you have offended God Who hath elected you for His adopted son; you have offended God Who hath made you an inheritor of paradise; you have offended God, the highest Good ----- goodness infinite ----- the fountain of grace; you have offended God while in the very act of blessing you.

Weep for your sins, because you have offended a God Who for love of you made Himself man; you have offended a God Who for love of you was born in a stable; you have offended a God Who, while yet in

His infancy, began to shed tears and Blood for you; you have offended a God Who for love of you lived poor and unknown in a workman's shed; you have offended a God Who for love of you went about preaching His heavenly doctrine amid toil and misery; you have offended a God Who for love of you instituted the most holy Sacraments; you have offended a God Who for love of you has left Himself to be entirely yours in the Most Holy Sacrament; you have offended a God Who sweated Blood for love of you; you have offended a God Who let Himself be bound and dragged and outraged for love of you; you have offended a God Who caused Himself to be buffeted, to be spit upon, to be kicked again and again, for love of you; you have offended a God Who chose to be tied to a pillar, and scourged, for love of you; you have offended a God Who chose to be crowned with thorns for love of you; you have offended a God Who let Himself be robed as a mock king, and made an object of jest and ridicule, for love of you; you have offended a God Who let Himself be loaded with a heavy Cross for love of you; you have offended a God Who caused His Hands and His Feet to be pierced with great nails for love of you; you have offended a God Who gave His last gasp hanging nailed on a Cross for love of you; you have offended a God Who let gall and vinegar be given to Him to drink for love of you; you have offended a God Who for a last pledge of His unbounded love, left you as a son to Mary, and Mary as mother to you; you have offended a God Who died transfixed upon a Cross for your salvation; you have offended a God Who let His Side be broken through by a spear for love of you; you have offended a God Who chose to be buried in a tomb; you have offended a God Who rose again to life, and sits at the right hand of the Father, to give Paradise to you; you have offended Jesus Christ your Redeemer, your Master, your Life, the Physician of your soul; you have offended a God Who hath tried hard by infinite kindness to get loved by you; you have offended a God Who seeks no recompense for so many benefits, Out only to be loved in return by you, and obeyed by you; you have offended a God Who seeks after your love in order to make you happy in this life, and, oh, how happy in the next! You have offended a God Who loves you as the pupil of His eye. My soul, my soul, you have done ill ----- and you could bear to do so! What harm had your God done to you? Tell me why you have offended Him. Begin now at least

102

to lament your sins, and to love God.

Oh, if I had always loved and served that God Who has loved me more than His own life! My love, my life, my salvation, my hope! I love Thee above all things, with my whole heart; I detest my sins more than any sort of affliction. I will confess my sins, and I wish never again to offend Thee, O my dear Redeemer!

Prayer Before Confession

O most loving Trinity, and most worthy of all love, Father, Son, and Holy Spirit, my God, I adore Thee. Behold this wretched creature at Thy feet, who desires to make his peace with Thee by means of a good Confession. But since, O my God, without Thy help I can do nothing but evil, I beseech of Thee, by the bowels of Thy compassion, to grant me light, that I may recollect all my sins; make me to perceive the hideousness and the enormity of sin, so that I may abhor and detest it with all my heart. O my Jesus, Fountain of pity, I draw near to Thee that Thou mayest wash and cleanse me of my filth. O Sun of justice, illuminate this poor blind creature. O Divine Physician, heal this poor sick man. O infinite Love, inflame this soul with Thy love, so that it may break down and dissolve in tears of grief. And may this my confession be such that I may now in earnest change my life, and never again find myself separated from Thee, my God my hope, my love, the salvation, life, and peace of my poor soul!

Prayer After Confession

Dear Jesus, be Thou forever blessed, for having by Thy pardon freed me from Hell, and replaced me in my inheritance of Paradise. Infinite Goodness, I thank Thee. But, O my God, I am capable of betraying Thee more than ever, and worse than Judas: I cannot trust to myself. Help, help me with Thy grace; hold Thy hands above me; help me in my temptations, and, oh, far rather take away my life than let me again offend Thee!

The Mass of St. Gregory by Adriaen Isenbrandt, no date

Exercises in Preparation for Holy Communion

*A*ise, my soul; revive thy faith, which tells thee that thy God beco-me man, that same Jesus Who was born in the stable of Bethlehem, that Jesus Who rose triumphant from the grave, that Jesus Who now sits glorious at the right hand of the Father, is now present with thee in the Most Holy Sacrament. O Faith! O Faith! what greater thing can be said and believed? God is here, in order to enter my heart and become entirely mine ----- the Almighty: God!

Act of Faith

My Jesus, Thou Truth infallible, since it is part of Thy revelation, I believe that Thou art present, Soul, Body, and Divinity, in the consec-rated host. I believe that in Communion I receive the same Jesus Who died, and Who rose again; and that in Him I receive the Father and the Holy Spirit.

Act of Adoration

O my soul, what art thou about? What thoughts engage thee? In a few minutes, thy God will enter within thee! O God, I profoundly humble myself, and I adore Thee. I adore Thee, beloved Jesus, in the Sacra-ment. Most holy Virgin, ye Angels, Saints, and Souls who love God, adore with me my Jesus; make up for my defect of worship, beseech for me living faith and profound veneration, now that I approach and receive Jesus Christ.

What can be wanting to thee, O my soul, now that the Almighty comes to visit thee? He comes to illuminate thee, to unite Himself heart to heart with thee, in order to give thee a lively pledge of that glory which He keeps prepared for thee in Heaven. Up! arise! enlarge thy heart, increase thy confidence; know that so much as thou hath promised to hear thee, and, bound by His word, He can give thee every good thing;

it costs Him no more than the opening of His Hand. Thy Jesus is to thee as a Father; much He loveth thee, and wishes to bestow on thee every sort of benefit. Thy Jesus, who is faithful, hath promised to hear thee, and, bound by His word, He will do thee great favors. Well, then, to grow rich in soul you need only to seek His graces, and ardently to hope.

Act of Hope

My Jesus, my hope, confiding in Thy promises through the Blood which Thou hast shed for me, I hope, O Infinite Pity, I hope that in receiving Thee, Thou wilt sanctify my soul, and enkindle within it heavenly desires; so that I may live and die loving only Thee, O Infinite Good. Yes, O my dearest God, God of all my hopes, Sanctifier of souls, sanctify me.

What more could God do, in order to get loved by thee? God has made Himself man, was born in a stable, died upon a Cross and dwells in the Sacrament for love of thee. Nay, that infinite love invites thee to receive Him, calls thee to Himself with a desire so strong that He cannot endure thy delays. O ingenious devices of love! The great God of infinite beauty and majesty wishes this morning to confer upon me such a favor as He hath never bestowed on the seraphim. He purposes to come to dwell in my heart; He wishes to unite Himself to me. And thou, my soul, dost thou not burn and flame with love toward a God Who is all love toward thee?

Act of Love

O my Jesus, my love, God of my soul, how good Thou art, how loving, how every way dear and worthy to be loved! My God, I love Thee with all my soul, my life, my heart, my mind, and all my faculties and strength. I love Thee more than myself, Thou one object of all my desires, my beginning and my last end. O that I had infinite tongues with which to praise and bless Thee! O that I could at any sacrifice carry Thy most holy name through the world, to make Thee known and loved! O God! I would willingly waste myself away in labors for the love of Thee. I desire to burn with love, I desire to bless Thee, to

106

thank Thee, to love Thee, with the love that the most holy Mary bore to Thee; I desire to love Thee more than all created beings united. I love Thee, my Jesus, my treasure, my Father, my life, my hope, my Heaven. Spouse of my soul, I love Thee, because Thou deservest to be loved ----- because Thou art God! Ah, Lord! would that I were all love, would that I did nothing but love Thee! My soul, created by God to love God, love Him then, love thy God; my heart, which can find no peace or satisfaction out of God, drive from thee every mere earthly attachment, and give welcome to thy God. Ah, Mary, mother of holy love, obtain for me to love my God!

How shouldest thou burn, my soul, to receive a God of infinite purity, holiness, and majesty, thou who art an abyss of vice, ingratitude, and sins! Hast thou forgotten all thou hast done against thy God? Ah, how often hast thou been more cruel, more afflicting to Jesus than Calvary itself! Jesus has been crucified in thee, so often as thou hast mortally sinned.

Act of Contrition

Dear Lord Jesus, by my sins I have crowned Thee with thorns, I have nailed Thee on the Cross, I have given Thee gall to drink, I have pierced Thy side, I have put Thee to death! I am not worthy to live, far less to receive Thee. I deserve that the earth should swallow me, that Heaven should hurl thunderbolts on my head, that all created things should turn in anger upon me. But, O my God, how good Thou art! How often have I trodden under foot Thy Blood, insulted Thy name, dishonored Thy authority; yet not only dost Thou pardon me, but Thou art the first to propose to be at peace with me; and for an act of penitence, for one tear of grief and affection, Thou forgivest me all my sins, Thou replacest me in Thy favor, and Thou makest me anew Thy friend and Thy son. And this is God ----- that it is that is meant by God! Oh, how I rejoice when I think that Thou art God; that is, infinite liberality, infinite magnanimity, infinite fidelity, infinite love; an abyss of infinite glories, attributes, and perfections! It suffices to say that Thou art good and in giving Thyself to me Thou knowest how to ordain for Thy greater glory, and for the greater good of my soul, even my very bygone sins. Glory to Thee! Ah, I could wish to die of grief for having offended so good a God. I am sorry that I have offended Thee! Forgive me, O my Lord. I do not heed my own interest; I only desire that Thou, great God, shouldst be honored and glorified by me, without ever being again offended by me. Wash, O beloved Jesus, my soul with Thy blood, and make it become a fit abode for Thy Divine Majesty. O most holy Mary, obtain for me tears of true contrition.

My soul, thou art about to feed upon the blessed Body of Jesus. And hast thou well considered what thou art, and who God is? If thou wert a seraph of love, if thou hadst the love felt by all the Angels, the virtues of all the Saints, wouldst thou even then be worthy of even once receiving God?

An Act of Humility

Behold, O my Jesus, the hour is come when Thou shalt be put into the power of this great sinner. O have patience with me; endure me by the bowels of Thy compassion! Ah, Lord, Thou art that God before the splendor of Whose holiness heaven and earth vanish into nothing. I confess the truth, in looking at Thy Majesty and at my unworthiness; I am so confounded and ashamed, that I should wish to hide myself in the abyss of my own nothingness. Yes, I must needs approach to receive Thee, for Thou incitest and commandest me, and like a son, I must obey Thee, O my King. Let the seraphim make up, let the Saints make up, let Mary make up ----- above all, let Thine Own infinite goodness make up for all my shortcomings in right devotion and love. O Lord, if I do not deserve to receive Thee and to love Thee, Thou deservest to be received and loved by me!

Dispose of me for Thine Own honor, make me worthy of so great a favor, give me all that I am wanting in, make me altogether Thine.

The hour is come, my soul, the blessed moment is come, when thou hast to receive thy dearest Jesus. Behold the King of kings, behold the Lord of lords, behold the Friend, behold the Father, behold the Spouse, behold the Joy of Paradise, behold the delight of Heaven, behold thy God Himself, behold all the Most Holy Trinity in the Divine Sacrament! *Ecce Sponsus venit, exite obviam ei.* „Behold the Bridegroom cometh; go forth to meet Him." (St. Matt. xxv. 6). But how, my soul, how standest thou thus so frozen, without one burning desire to feed upon that Sacred Body? Ah! should not the overflowing of the Divine compassion all enkindle thee with love? And here Shepherd, guide me. Come, O my Father, my Spouse, my Treasure, my Life, my Bliss, and my Rest. Come, Thou one end of all my longings. Come, light of souls, refreshment of hearts, consoler of the sorrowing. Come, Thou expected One of all nations, sighed for by the holy patriarchs, desire of the eternal hills, joy of Angels, delight of Heaven, beatitude of the Saints. Come, O my Paradise: come, for I desire Thee, for I sigh after Thee. Come, art thou all frozen! If it wert to do only once in all thy life, with what fervor wouldst thou not do it! But now, while the Infinite Goodness waits ever ready at thy pleasure, thou goest up so tepid, so dull of heart, to receive a God so great! Enamoured souls have burned with desire of this Communion, and have run like thirsty stags to that fount Divine. Up, up, my soul; awake, kindle in thyself a most ardent longing to receive Jesus; sigh after that Supremest Good, desire Him, call on Him with tears and with sighs, and with a heart in flames of holy love.

An Act of Desire

Come, O thou Divine food, and nourish my hungry soul. Come, furnace of charity, and kindle me; come, flaming fire of love, inflame me by thy flames. Come, heavenly for Thou hast wounded me with love; come, delay not, for my heart is failing, and I feel that life would not be life without Thee. Arise for pity, O my Jesus, and come.

Most holy Virgin, already I am at hand, and about to receive thine and my Jesus. From thy hands I purpose to receive Him. Hold Him forth to me, as thou didst to the shepherds, and the holy kings and to holy Simeon. Prepare me to receive Him with love. Give Him to me quickly, and pray to Him to fill me with His dearest benediction; and do thou accompany it with thine.

An Act of Offering

I protest, O my God, that I purpose to unite this my Communion with the Communion of most holy Mary, of Thy Apostles, of Thy Saints, and of all the just who receive Thee this morning, or who shall ever receive Thee in time to come. My desire and purpose is, to make all their devout acts, all their preparations, all their thanksgivings; and I mean to offer the whole in union with those virtues, that merit, that holiness, with which Thou, O my Jesus, didst receive Thyself in the Sacrament, at the Last Supper. May the Church triumphant and militant now supply my defects of love, and worship, and thanks.

Defenders of the Eucharist by Peter Paul Rubens, 1577 - 1640

Devotions After Holy Communion

*B*ehold, my longings are fulfilled! Behold, my desires are satisfied! Now hath my God come to visit me! Now Jesus dwelleth within me! Now I am no longer my own but Christ's: I no longer live in myself, but in Jesus, and Jesus lives in me. I am altogether the possession of Jesus, and Jesus is altogether mine.

O Infinite Goodness! A God ----- the God of Heaven ----- hath touched the tongue, and come within the breast, and sought the heart of a human creature, and one so vile, so unworthy as I am! My soul, of what art thou thinking? Behold thyself now in possession of that for which thou hast been sighing; behold thyself all hallowed by the presence of Jesus, transformed into Jesus. Thou and Jesus art one. O union true and wonderful! My soul, my soul, art thou thus closely united to Jesus, and yet sayest nothing to Him, and speakest not with thy God Who is in thine arms, within thy breast, at thy heart? Up, up, arise, collect thyself, gather up all the affections of thy spirit; adore Him, and say to Him:

O welcome, dearest Jesus, to the mansion of my soul. Oh, how long have I desired this hour! But, oh, how I pity Thee, now that I see Thee placed in this heart, more hard and cold than the stall where thou wast born; a heart more full of what is grief and anguish to Thee than Calvary was to Thy sacred flesh; for not once, but a hundred, and a thousand times, have I renewed Thy death and Passion by my sins! Lord, what dost Thou find in me but hardness and obduracy against Thee, and affections all given to earthly things! Ah, my God, how is it Thou hast come to dwell in me? I must cry out with St. Peter, Depart from me, depart from me, O Majesty of God; depart from this soul of sin, which is not worthy to harbor God; *Exi a me, quia homo peccator sum, Domine.* (St. Luke v. 8). Go, and rest within those pure and fervent souls who welcome Thee so tenderly. But, no, O my most precious blessing; no, let it never be so; do not leave me, for if Thou art far from me, I am lost. O God, my hope, I will not let Thee go! O blessing, for which I have sighed, I press Thee to my heart, and I wish to live and die thus embracing Thee. O most holy Mary, O Angels, Saints, and Souls that love your God! lend me your affections, that I may fitly welcome and cherish this presence of my Jesus.

Act of Thanksgiving

O Divine Trinity, one God, most worthy to be loved, I thank Thee from the very depth of my heart, because Thou hast given me Jesus; I thank Thee because Thou hast left me Jesus in the Sacrament; I thank Thee for having caused me to receive Him; I thank Thee, my Jesus, that Thou hast deigned to visit me. O God, what return can I make for so much love! How can I thank Thee enough, O most holy Virgin, O Angels, O Saints of Heaven, O all enamoured Souls, help me to thank our God, to thank and thank Him again and again, for this infinite kindness. But, O God, how little even is all this! The thanksgiving of all Paradise cannot attain to be thanks sufficient to an infinite God, or recommend Him for His benefits. What, then, shall I do? I know not, except, O my most holy Jesus, to offer up Thine Own love itself in thanks for Thine infinite love. May Thine infinite compassion, Thy kindness, and all the abyss of Thine infinite attributes, render to Thee that honor and that thank-offering which Thou deservest. O Most Holy Trinity, one God, I thank Thee by the hands of Jesus; and do Thou, O Triune God, thank Jesus for me! And now let my heart remain full, and let Thy Majesty accept and be satisfied with these infinite thanks. O my Blessing, to Thee alone be praise, glory, and honor from all creatures, forever and forever. Amen.

What art thou doing, my soul? Dost thou know that now thou art a living temple in which really dwells thy Redeemer? It is no time now for lying slothful, and full of wandering thoughts. It is the time for asking all the graces of which thou standest in need, and for receiving them from the true and living God Who is dwelling within thee.

Now the heavens stand open, now the Most Holy Trinity, with eyes all full of love, is above thee, looking down on the object of Its own complacency ----- Jesus Christ, Who is within thy breast. Now more than ever Mary, and Angels, and Saints, thy advocates, are beseeching graces for thee from God. My soul, my soul, lose not of these precious moments; bend thy faculties to deal with the great affair of thy eternal salvation. But how? Art thou saying nothing to thy God? Ah, poor and miserable as thou art, thou delightest to live on amid thy miseries, while thou hast with Thee the God of all riches; and thou art silent, and thy mind begins already to wander, and thou art so without desire of interest, so dull and so idle of heart! Dost thou not know that if thou seekest not thou obtainest not? Were a king to enter thy house and invite thee to ask favors of him, wouldst thou be long silent? Ah, miserable race, through our little faith! The King of kings, with His royal presence, is within thee, the Lord of the heavenly treasures. A God ----- thy God ----- hath come to thee, Who wishes to bestow great graces on thee and thou speakest not a word! This Infinite Benignity grieves and laments that His favors are not sought; and, unable longer to endure the languid and indifference of men, forever longing to be kind to them and do them good, He Himself takes to inviting them, and beseeches them to ask. *Usque modo non petistis quidquam in nomine meo. Petite, et accipietis, ut gaudium vestrum sit plenum* (St. John XVI. 24). My soul, thou hast within thee a Lord omnipotent, a most loving and munificent Father, a most faithful God: and of what art thou afraid? Seek and confide, enlarge thy heart, revive thy faith; begin, ask great graces ----- heavenly graces, graces worthy of God.

Act of Petition

O my dear Redeemer, since Thou hast come to me, in order to confer graces upon me, and invitest me to ask them of Thee, hear me now by the bowels of Thy compassion. Give me, O my Jesus, an increase of living faith, hope, charity, and contrition. Give me humility, purity, patience, and all virtues; take from me all my corruptions. Change this heart, so full of the world and of myself, and give me a new heart conformed to Thy will, so that I may always seek Thy greater glory, and that all its affections may aspire to Thee and aim only at Thy love, without ever deviating even in the very least. *Cor mundum crea in me Deus, et spiritum rectum innova in visceribus meis* (Ps. 1. 12). Grace is indeed a mighty gift, and though I merit it not, Thou meritest it for me. From a great and glorious God great favors may be sought; grant me this, then, which I have asked, by Thy Passion, by Thy death; grant

114

it by the love Thou bearest to the Eternal Father; grant it me by the virtue of most holy Mary, by all the merits of the Church triumphant and militant; grant it me because Thou art Thyself infinite goodness and mercy.

Here apply yourself to ask with lively faith from God the graces and favors which are needful for yourself and your neighbor.

O Most Holy Trinity, O my omnipotent God, hear these my prayers. Now is not the time to refuse graces even to the most unworthy, because it is not I myself alone that am seeking them, but, together with me, Jesus Christ is supplicating. Though I do not deserve to be heard, Jesus Christ deserves it, Who prays with me, and in me, and for me. Eternal Father, I call up before Thee the promises of Jesus Christ, Who hath said that whatever graces we seek from Thee in His name, without any other means, they shall be obtained from Thee: *Amen amen, dico vobis, si quid petieritis Patrem in nomine meo, dabit vobis* (St. John XVI. 23).

Act of Oblation

My Jesus, it is but justice and common gratitude that I should give myself entirely to Thee, after Thou hast given Thyself entirely to me. Thou hast, in coming to me, penetrated and made godlike all my being with Thy Divinity, and so I ought henceforward to continue Thine. May these eyes, renewed by Thee, continue Thine; may these ears, sanctified by Thee, continue Thine; this taste, sanctified by Thee, may it be Thine. Thou hast sanctified all my senses; may they be Thine, and so may they never again take pleasure in opposition to Thy Divine Law. Thou hast sanctified my memory; may it continually remember Thee. Thou hast sanctified my will; may it never turn to love anything in preference to Thee. Unto Thee, then, from the very depth of my heart, I offer, as a perpetual holocaust, my body and my soul, my senses and my faculties, all that I have and am, as fully as I can. Burn, O fire Divine, bum and consume, O love omnipotent, all in me which is not Thine! Amen.

PORTRAIT OF THE TRUE CHRISTIAN

*T*know the Catholic religion, to respect it, to love it, to avoid diligently that which it prohibits, to fulfill exactly that which it commands.

To believe in God, to hope in Him, to love Him, to pray often to Him, to thank Him, to praise Him, to adore Him, to fear Him, to submit perfectly to Him.

To observe subordination, piety, justice, goodness, charity toward our superiors, or equals, and our inferiors.

To be humble, teachable, patient, modest, chaste, temperate, detached from the world and from self, and to be occupied about our own salvation, and the means of attaining it.

All this to be fulfilled with the intention of rendering glory to God, in faithful imitation of Jesus Christ, His Son, our Lord, our Head, and our Model.

This is the portrait of a true Christian. Seek to make it your own.

The Feeding of the Five Thousand by Hendrix De Clerck, no date

117

Act of Oblation To Be Made Every Morning

Eternal God, and my God, behold me prostrate before Thine immense Majesty, and humbly adoring Thee. I offer Thee all my thoughts, words, and actions of this day. I purpose them all to be thought, spoken, and done entirely for love of Thee, for Thy glory, to fulfill Thy Divine will, to serve Thee, praise Thee, and bless Thee; in order also to my own enlightenment in the mysteries of the holy Faith, for the securing of my salvation, and out of hope in Thy loving mercy; for satisfaction, too, of Thy Divine justice, for my so many and most grievous sins; as supplication for the Holy Souls in Purgatory, and for the grace of a true conversion to all sinners; in fine, I wish and intend to do everything in union with the most pure intentions of Jesus and Mary during their lives on earth, of all the Saints who are in Heaven, and of all the just who are on earth: and I would willingly subscribe to this my intention with my own blood, and to repeat it from a loving heart, as often as there are moments in eternity. Receive, O my dearest God, this my good intention; give me Thy holy benediction with efficacious grace to keep me from mortal sin through all my life, but particularly this day, in which I desire and purpose to receive all the Indulgences which I am capable of receiving, and to assist, were it possible, at all the Masses which are celebrated this day throughout the whole world, applying all in supplication for the Holy Souls in Purgatory, that they may be freed from detention in its pains and come quickly before the face of God. So be it.

Act of Supplication to Obtain of God the General Pardon of Sins and Every Other Gift Consistent with Eternal Salvation

*O*my omnipotent God, Who art infinite in all Thy admirable attributes, but art especially rich in compassion, and art ever urged by that love of Thine, by which Thou so liberally grantest what we humbly and with lively faith petition for; Who art also faithful ----- oh, yes, most faithful ----- in fulfilling Thy promises, I, Thy miserable creature, in order to obtain the grace of a general pardon of my sins, and the supply of all my other necessities, declare my firm belief that Thou art able, and art willing, and knowest how to grant me so great a grace. And, together with this faith, I hope with a most firm reliance, efficacious desire, certain confidence, and unhesitating trust, that Thou wilt grant it to me. With this true and firm confidence, which I repose in Thee and in Thy promises, I hope and wish for this perfect pardon, this very moment in which I am humbly beseeching it, in which I am here sighing that my soul may be purified from all the stains of my grievous sins. These sins I abominate and detest from pure love of Thee, and because they are opposed to Thy supreme perfection and goodness.

My God, my God, be moved to compassion. I ask of Thee with a holy courage, founded on the infinite merits of my Lord Jesus Christ, which merits through Thy great loving kindness have become mine, that Thou wouldst permit me to apply to my soul the grace of a thorough and intimate pardon of my sins; I ask it, and I trust indeed to get the grace which I ask. And since a grace so glorious as that of the pardon of sin tends and is ordained to Thy greater glory, as well as the spiritual good of my soul, I believe, I trust through Thy most loving fidelity, justice, omnipotence, and benignity, that Thou dost will, even at this very time, to grant it me; while I, as Thy poor creature, do hereby accept of it, and with my whole will take it to myself for pure love of Thee. O my God, before Whose face I stand, I protest that I am determined never more to sin, and I most humbly beseech Thee that now, having granted the general pardon of my sins, Thou wouldst chain all evil spirits in the depth of the abyss, so as never more to have the courage nor the power to draw away either me or others from Thy Divine service.

See me now, my dearest God, free, as I hope, from the bonds of my hateful sins. Animated by this sweet hope, I trust to live and die in the arms of Thy Divine compassion. That compassion I will invoke every moment. Every moment I mean that this blessed petition for pardon of past sin, and for help never more to sin, shall be renewed; my will and wish is that it should go on forever, my mouth uttering from my heart those most sweet words:

O my Jesus, compassion! Compassion, O my Jesus!

I wish to live with these blessed words upon my tongue, and to die with these holy words stamped upon my heart. I wish to say them a hundred, and a thousand times a day.

Compassion, O my Jesus! O my Jesus, compassion!

The Christ Child: the Good Shepherd by Murillo, 1665

Chapter 6

Rules for Living Well

*H*e who desires to be saved, lives according to rule, and establishes an arrangement of his time with a view to devotional exercises. Dearest reader, if you wish to maintain yourself in the grace of God, never abandon these brief exercises which I now propose to you.

Choose for yourself a good confessor, to whom you may confide the treasure of your soul. Go often to him, to give an account of your conscience, and do not change him by mere caprice or fickleness.

Every morning offer to the Lord all the good works of that day, all its labors and sufferings, and all your actions, in union with the merits of Jesus Christ.

Offer all your actions to the Most Holy Trinity, to Mary, ever Virgin, and to all the blessed of Heaven, in suffrage for the Souls in Purgatory.

Form the intention to gain the Indulgences obtainable by prayer or act during the whole day.

Avoid sloth, bad company, dangerous conversations, and games; remembering that time passes and never returns, that you have a soul, and that if you lose your soul, you lose all.

EVERY MORNING

When as yet scarcely awake, give your very first thought to God; while dressing keep reciting vocal prayers, and recommend yourself to God ----- then say upon your knees: „Most Holy Trinity, I believe that Thou art present with me; and I adore Thee. I thank Thee for having preserved me during the past night; I offer to Thee all my actions. My God, my love, Goodness Infinite, and worthy of all love, assist me this day; keep me free from sins and dangers; hold Thy hands above me, and preserve me from betraying Thee.

Then say three *Glorias* to the Most Holy Trinity, one *Pater* to Jesus, three *Aves* to Mary, and beseech her to guard you under her mantle; offer all your senses and faculties to Jesus and Mary.

Act of Faith

O my God, Infallible Truth, I believe all that Holy Church teaches, because Thou hast revealed it. I believe in the Most Holy Trinity, Father, Son, and Holy Spirit, three Persons, and one God, Who punishes the wicked, and rewards the good. I believe that the eternal Son of God made Himself man, and died to save my soul; that He rose again from the dead, exists in Heaven, and in the Most Blessed Sacrament; bears the name Jesus Christ; is the Judge of the living and the dead; and that it is He Who instituted the holy Sacraments as means of pardon and sanctification. I thank Thee that Thou hast made me a Catholic. Grant me the grace that I may live and die entirely Thine, and ever exclaiming, O blessed faith of Jesus Christ!

Act of Hope

My God, my hope, my ever faithful God, mighty and compassionate, trusting in Thy promises, I hope to obtain from Thee, through the Blood of Jesus Christ, the pardon of my sins, the virtues of sanctity, and the glories of Paradise.

Act of Charity

My God, my love, Father, and Spouse of my soul, Supreme and Infinite Good, I love Thee with my whole heart, because Thou art worthy of all love. I love Thee more than my life, and for love of Thee I love my neighbor as myself. O God, would that I could love Thee as the seraphs love Thee. Would that I were able at the cost of my blood, to make all the world to know and to love Thee.

Act of Contrition

O God, my beloved, Thou hast created me to love and to serve Thee, and I, ungrateful, have done nothing but offended Thee. I am confounded; I repent. Infinite Goodness, would that I had never offended Thee! Would that I might die of sorrow! Pardon me, my Jesus, by the Blood which Thou hast shed for me! I promise to love Thee forever, and never to repulse Thee by sin again.

Then make a half-hour's mental prayer, or at least during quarter of an hour, upon the Passion of Jesus, and upon the last things, death and judgment.

Never omit to hear holy Mass every morning [It is not always possible, given the modern situation, unknown when the Saint wrote this treatise ------ -the Web Master.]. It is an infinite treasure, and will be infinitely profitable to you.

Afterward you will go to your affairs, often recalling your thoughts to God, Who is ever present beside you.

At table give a thought to God, and act upon the resolution of eating in order to live and serve your God. Practise some little mortification at each meal. Then thank the Lord.

In the Course of each Day

Give a short time to prayer; visit the Most Holy Sacrament and our Blessed Lady. Read some devout book, and do some good to your neighbor. Recite five *Paters*, *Aves*, and *Glorias* to the wounds of Jesus, and beseech Him to pardon your sins, remove your corruptions, and bestow upon you virtues; that He may grant you perseverance, and fit you for Paradise. Repeat also three *Paters*, *Aves*, and *Glorias* to the Most Holy Trinity, with three acts of love, in gratitude for the graces granted to Mary, to the Saints, and to yourself. Recite devoutly the third part of the most holy *Rosary*, with Litanies. When you meet acquaintances, use for salutation, All praise to Jesus Christ and Mary! and in reply, Forever! You will thus gain many Indulgences.

In the midst of your work or business, lift up your mind from time to time to that God Who is ever present with you. Collect your thoughts, and with some short prayers recommend yourself often to Him.

Every Evening

If you are head of a family, collect your household. Join with them in prayers for a short time, and then say the most holy Rosary with them. Before going to bed, examine your conscience thus:

1. Place yourself in the presence of God, and thank Him for all the benefits received from Him, more especially those of the bygone day.

2. Entreat for light to know your sins, and for graces whereby to amend.

3. Examine yourself as to the sins of the day.

4. Ask pardon of God with all your heart, and promise never more to offend Him, and to fly from all the occasions which have proved themselves most dangerous to you.

5. Pray to the Lord to protect you during the coming night, and offer

every breath you draw as an aspiration to Jesus.

6. Repeat three *Aves* to Mary, and a *Pater* in honor of your Angel Guardian. Repeat the acts of Faith, Hope, Charity, and Contrition, already given.

Sleep with some holy picture or image near you.

Let no worldly thought enter or remain in your mind. If you wake, pray to Jesus, and invoke Mary.

EVERY WEEK

Receive with all devotion the Most Holy Sacrament. Give a sincere account of your conscience to your spiritual Father. Frequent some devout congregation or confraternity of Mary. Fast or practise some abstinence beyond the law of the Church on Friday or Saturday.

EVERY MONTH

Choose some of the Saints, or some choir of Angels, for special advocates during it. Select some special virtue in which particularly to exercise yourself. Go into retirement during one day, in order particularly to revise and probe your conscience. Undertake to discover your dominant passion, and lay down for yourself particular methods for overcoming it. Prepare during that day for dying well; arrange for the departure of your soul; make a most exact confession, and all those solemn protests of entire submission, devoted resignation, of generous confidence, of ardent desire, of prostrate penitence, of faith, of hope, of charity, and all the supernatural acts of the soul, which befit the dying Catholic.

Go through the spiritual exercises during eight days, attending only to God and your soul. Make a general confession, and determine on the details of a more effective pursuit of a holy course of life during the remainder of your days on earth.

ST. LEONARD, PRAY FOR US.